Alaska History No. 44

CLOTHING IN COLONIAL RUSSIAN AMERICA: *A NEW LOOK*

by
John Middleton

edited by
Lyn Kalani

The Limestone Press
Kingston, Ontario : Fairbanks, Alaska
1996

Box 1604
Kingston, Ontario K7L 3N6
Canada

U.S. Office:
The Limestone Press
℅ History Department
University of Alaska Fairbanks
Fairbanks, Alaska 99775-0860
U.S.A.

Distributed by University of Alaska Press.
P. O. Box 756240
Fairbanks, Alaska 99775-6240

International Standard Book Number 1-895901-08-1

CONTENTS

TITLE PAGE: SEAL OF THE RUSSIAN-AMERICAN COMPANY

PREFACE

With increasing interest in Russian America, many sources now unpublished will undoubtedly soon be available; and these, I hope, will update the information collected for this study. Clothing is a very important part of the material culture of any society, and the study of its use will add to our understanding of that society.

Much of any attempt to reconstruct the attire of an entire colony must be based largely on supposition. I have tried, in presenting accounts from lists and from the written record, to establish the appearance of people of whom we have little pictorial evidence.

I would gratefully accept evidence that would correct any misconceptions found here, and will welcome any new sources that would shed more light on a very obscure subject.

❖ ❖ ❖

ACKNOWLEDGEMENTS

I gratefully acknowledge the assistance of the following, who very kindly provided the information and sources for much of this work: Sherry Madrone and Richard Bradley of the Fort Ross Interpretive Association Costume Committee, who assisted with proofreading and the compilation of illustrations for the first draft of the manuscript; the Board of Directors of the Fort Ross Interpretive Association which provided the author with grants for two research trips to the U.S.S.R. in 1989 and 1990; Svetlana Fedorova, Alexei Istomin, and the late Sergei Serov of the Institute of Anthropology and Ethnography, Moscow, Russia; Viktor Malyshev of the State Artillery History Museum, St. Petersburg, Russia; Captain Evgeny N. Korchagin of the Central Naval Museum, St. Petersburg, Russia; Oleg Terichow, Nikolai Rokitiansky, Shirley Jolliff, and Mark and Midori Hanus of the Fort Ross Interpretive Association; William Walton, Glenn Farris, William and Diane Pritchard, Glenn Burch and Jeanette Schultz of the California Department of Parks and Recreation; Richard Pierce of the University of Alaska, Fairbanks, Lynne Goldstein of the University of Wisconsin-Milwaukee and Stephen Watrous of Sonoma State University.

I especially thank Lyn Kalani, without whose continued encouragement and gentle prodding this book would never have been written. The format and detailed construction of the book are entirely to her credit and editorial abilities.

SETTLEMENT ROSS, 1841
I. G. Voznesenskii

INTRODUCTION

Clothing in Colonial Russian America: A New Look was written primarily to study the clothing worn at Ross, the Russian-American Company's colony in California from 1812 to 1841. The majority of quotes in the text refer to the colonies in Alaska, but with the close connection via company ships, the material culture of both the colonial administration's center in New Archangel and its southern settlement in California was quite similar. Two recent museum exhibitions, translations of articles in rare Russian journals, at the same time as the publication of several magazine articles on Fort Ross and Russian America in American periodicals, the Fort Ross cemetery restoration project, and the opening of Russian archives over the last five years have provided better understanding of life at this Russian colony. This information, while adding to and in many cases supporting accounts already known, alters or casts doubt upon other ideas we have held as true. The purpose of this "new look" is to supply the reader with information based on this new material, and illustrate the descriptions with original works or studies, whenever possible, rather than re-drawn illustrations that may lose some slight detail that is necessary to understanding. Illustrations in this study primarily portray clothing of the 1820s through the 1840s.

The question of costumes that are historically accurate for Russian America, and in particular Fort Ross, is a difficult one. In contrast to other historic sites that are well documented, illustrated in contemporary works, or which may even have original examples of period clothing, Fort Ross has virtually nothing. There are a few drawings, two or three by I.G. Voznesenskii of inhabitants of California who may or may not be Russians, one by Duflot de Mofras of a Russian in the doorway of his house, and several fine watercolors by M. Tikhanov depicting the native peoples near the settlement. These works, combined with a few artifacts in poor condition from archaeological finds in the fort and vicinity, provide what little information can be obtained to reconstruct clothing for an entire colony which included Russians (Finns, Balts, Ukrainians, and Cossacks) Asiatic Siberians, Pacific Islanders, Alaskans and California Natives, and Creoles, the children of Russian men and native North American women.

Russian costume varied greatly according to class. This study has been divided into four basic groups, roughly corresponding to the class (estate) structure of Imperial Russian administration. The first group, ***ADMINISTRATORS***, will include managers, assistants, and clerks in the administration of the colony. ***TOWNSMEN AND CREOLES*** form the second group, ***LABORERS***, group three, and ***NAVY AND MERCHANT SHIPPERS*** group four. This last chapter will contain a cross section of all class members, with officers, petty officers and seamen, corresponding to gentry, townsmen and peasant class. A series of drawings by Viktor N. Malyshev, which were completed as part of his internship at Fort Ross in 1991 are included. They represent reconstructions of costume mentioned in the literature. As Conservator of Collections in the State Artillery History Museum, St. Petersburg, Russia, and consultant to the State Museum of Ethnography and the Central Navy Museum, both in St. Petersburg, Viktor systematically measured, recorded, and illustrated details of civil and military costumes, concentrating on the periods of Aleksandr I and Nikolai I (1801-1855). Viktor's research represents clothing particularly available in the colonies, and clearly records the differences in class hierarchy. Readers are encouraged to refer to the original published work for clothing details that may not be clear in the work's reproductions.

PART I
ADMINISTRATORS

DECEMBRISTS 1830s - 1840s, N. A. Bestuzhev

ADMINISTRATORS

Two portraits painted in Russian America give concrete evidence of types of clothing worn in the colonies during the first half of the nineteenth century. This is extremely fortunate for the researcher of Russian costume in America, for as noted before, very little pictorial evidence exists. The two portraits are of the most important figures in the founding of Fort Ross, Aleksandr A. Baranov, chief administrator of the colonies, and Ivan A. Kuskov, administrator of Fort Ross.

ALEXANDER BARANOV
Lithograph after an oil,
Mikhail T. Tikhanov

Both men are portrayed in uniform. In each case it is the uniform of the civil service of Imperial Russia. Baranov's portrait, painted in 1818 by Mikhail Tikhanov shows the chief administrator wearing the undress uniform (Ryndina; 1961; 98,102) with the Order of St. Anna, Second Class, at his neck. Baranov was initially sent a uniform in 1803, in recognition of his receiving the medal "For Zealous Service" (Zagoskin; 1967; 68,76). That uniform would have been the same as the one in which Kuskov is pictured, and reflects the status of a member of the merchant class. Upon receipt of the Order of St. Anna, Baranov was elevated to the ranks of the nobility, and received a position on the "Table of Ranks" of Peter the First. At that time the Order of St. Anna conferred upon its recipients hereditary nobility (Werlich; 1981; 15). Suspended from the button on the right side of Baranov's black-green coat is a medal for the campaign in 1812 against Napoleon. Members of the merchant class could receive this medal for contributions to the patriotic cause. There was also a full dress and frock coat version available to civil servants, and strict regulations governing their use were published annually in the *Polnoe sobranie zakonov* or *Complete Collection of Laws* (Ryndina; 1961; 98).

CIVIL SERVICE UNIFORMS
Ink wash drawing,
V. Kozlinskii

Lavrentii Zagoskin, writing in Novoarkangel'sk in 1842, described in some detail Baranov's use of his uniform. "If some pronouncement had to be made public as, for instance, the punishment of some person as an example to others, or new agreements with the natives or with the captains of ships from the United States, he would on such occasions array himself in the uniform which had been sent him in 1803, and come forth onto a platform which was no more than three sazhen square and which is still today called The Parade." It appears then, that the use of a uniform, civil or military, was practiced for official purposes from the very beginning.

The portraits of I. A. Kuskov and his wife are surrounded with some controversy. Some scholars believe that because of an inscription on the reverse of Kuskov's portrait it was painted at Fort Ross. The frames, apparently made of California redwood, supported this theory. However, more recent scholars believe this doubtful; indeed there may even be some doubt that the portraits are of the Kuskovs (Fedorova; 1979; 243), (Pierce; 1990; 285). The portraits show the couple in clothing typical for a merchant class family in government service in the first quarter of the nineteenth century in Russia. "The single breasted coat of a commercial counsellor, almost black (such a shade was formerly called dark-green broadcloth) with a standing collar, small shoulder straps with gilded buttons, a buckle on a row of large gilt buttons, a golden sword knot at his waist; on his left arm is a sword, and on his chest, hanging on a short St. Vladimir's ribbon, is a gold medal." (Fedorova; 1979; 238) Ekaterina Kuskova is shown in a "cream colored, slightly low-necked dress in the empire style, edged with lace and a blue belt which encloses her waistline (in the early 19th century fashion). On her shoulders is wrapped a cream colored shawl with a broad border (a large floral decoration on a dark red background), three strings of pearls on her smooth neck, and pearl earrings are on her ears." (Fedorova; 1979; 244) The portraits are particularly interesting for Fort Ross. If they were indeed painted in Russian America, they give strong evidence to the high standard of living mentioned by other eye witness accounts, and support the notion that the Russians retained the traditions of the homeland in dress and social structure as well as in architecture.

IVAN A. KUSKOV
Oil on cardboard,
artist unknown

The wives and daughters of the administrators seemed to follow very closely the fashions of the motherland. The wife of a commerce counsellor of the merchant class, Ekaterina Prokhorovna, appears in clothing of the ladies' fashion in Europe and Russia of the same period. Zagoskin also mentions this apparent social climbing with creole women. (Zagoskin; 1967; 68) Social distinctions between the merchant classes and the nobility were occasionally blurred as concerns costume. Provincial merchants tended to prefer a more conservative look in both dress and appearance, whereas the merchants of the cities often dressed very much like ladies and gentlemen. Lest one think that these fashions applied only to the Russian American capital, Zagoskin writes that even at the Fort Kolmakov outpost a native named Kantelnuk dressed himself "in full European dress, that is, in shirt, breeches, and cap." (Zagoskin; 1967; 233) The type of cloth (less expensive and perhaps more gaudy) and small details

EKATERINA P. KUSKOVA
Oil on cardboard,
artist unknown

PORTRAIT OF A MERCHANT WITH TWO MEDALS ON THE NECK
V. A. Tropinin, 1838

of construction were usually the only indications. (Malyshev; 1991) Rules which forbade members of one estate wearing the clothing of a higher class seem only to have been applied in the most extreme cases (peasant - gentry), much as we now have laws for impersonating authority. This applies only in cases where the lower class wanted to appear in the clothing of an upper class. It was a popular pastime for members of the gentry to wear costumes "in the national style" (Petinova; 1987; pl.53) and often to dress their servants in peasant costume. The study of women's fashions in Russian America is not a difficult one as concerns the upper classes. They appear to be consistent with contemporary European style, as were those in Russia. They certainly seemed to be up to date, as in Kuskova's painting.

BARONESS ELIZABETH VON WRANGELL

Except for the two uniforms mentioned above, which were evidently worn for official occasions, there are several accounts of the type of civilian clothing worn in the colonies. Another passage on Baranov mentions him wearing "a raspberry colored frock coat of Utrecht velvet for "important holidays". (Zagoskin; 1967; 68) The frock coat at that period was worn by members of the townsmen (*meshchanin*) estate as well as merchants and gentry. There were some minor details which distinguished the two, slight variations in construction and quality of cloth. (Malyshev; 1991) There was a distinct difference in dress between those involved in colonial administration and the workers. Zagoskin mentions that it "has only been literacy that has made it possible for a member of the working class in Novoarkangel'sk to effect the change from the long English jacket to the frock coat and the rank of clerk." (Zagoskin; 1967; 102) V.M. Golovnin in 1818 remarked that in the company settlements "you will not see a single official who would resemble a military man; all of them are clad in dress coats, jackets, and frock coats." S. G. Fedorova states that "In Nicholas I's time, when everyone in service in Russia went about in uniform, the company personnel in Russian America wore "civil" clothing, and this peculiarity was striking to all observers." (Fedorova; 1973; 231) The discrepancy between the pictorial and written record can be explained. Golovnin mentions "military man" in his notes. Military uniforms were quite elaborate in 1818, compared to the civil service uniforms of the period. Except for the gilt brass buttons on the undress uniform worn in the Baranov portrait, there is nothing to distinguish it from a civilian tail coat, except for the official color. The cocked hats and caps undistinguished without braid and cockades were not unknown to civil dress.

GOVERNOR FERDINAND P. VON WRANGELL

Without the shakos, gold braided epaulets and galloon embroidery, civil service uniforms were very un-military indeed. Whereas it seems that the majority of the employees in administrative positions did wear "civil dress", it is also clear that the executives of the settlements appeared in civil service uniform for official acts.

On February 1, 1818 Fleet Lieutenant L. A. Hagemeister of the Imperial Russian Navy replaced A. A. Baranov as the chief administrator of the Russian colonies in America. Thereafter, all the governors of Russian America were serving naval officers. During the reign of Nikolai I in Russia, officers in military service were required to wear the uniform at all times, even when off duty (Troyat; 1979; 121) All portraits of governors prior to 1859 depict them in their naval uniform. It must be pointed out that none of these portraits were painted while the portrayed served in Russian America as governor. The only first-hand views of Sitka, painted by a Japanese drifter (castaway) in 1842, depict the governor in a uniform frock coat with epaulets. (Plummer; 1991; 72,76) Given Jirokichi's unfamiliarity with western artistic and cultural traditions, it is surprising to note his accuracy in recalling details of costume some three years after observation. (Plummer; 1991; X1) The epaulets on the frock coat indicate a military or naval uniform, as the civil service uniform never carried these. (Zlatich; 1963; letter) Captain-Lieutenant F. P. Litke noted in Sitka in 1827 that "naval officers are always in uniform" (1987; 53), which was later confirmed by Jirokichi's drawings.

Aside from the executives, colonial administrators were mostly clerks, (*prikashchiki*), foremen (*artelshchiki*), team leaders (*baidarshchiki*) and captains of Company ships. After Kuskov and Baranov the ranking of their positions rose so that by the time of Rotchev (1838-41) the position of administrator at Fort Ross was held by a gentleman, his wife a princess. The clerks and foremen however, tended to remain within the townsman estate, and their clothing, while evidently of a type that would suggest a higher class, remained essentially the clothing of the lower middle class of other countries.

L.A. HAGEMEISTER
Oil on canvas,
artist unknown

MARGARETHA ETHOLEN
Oil on canvas,
J. E. Lindh, 1839

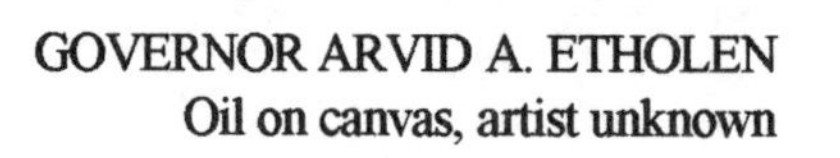

GOVERNOR ARVID A. ETHOLEN
Oil on canvas, artist unknown

AT THE CASTLE
Ink on paper, watercolor, Jirokichi, 1842

PART II
TOWNSMEN AND CRE0LES

A CREOLE, CALIFORNIA
I. G. Voznesenskii, 1841

TOWNSMEN AND CREOLES

Townsmen (*meshchanie*) occupied a position on the Imperial Russian social scale which approximated the petit bourgeoisie or lower middle class of other countries. They were free men in a country which practiced serfdom, and could travel and live throughout the empire as their passports permitted. The majority were occupied as tradesmen, craftsmen, clerks, and in the numerous occupations that cities and towns provided. In the Russian-American Company they served in the lower to middle managerial positions or were artisans, often acting as foremen for the occupations required to support the colonies. If one combines their number with those of the creoles, they made up the majority of the population at the Ross colony. (Petrov; 1988; 64)

Creoles were the offspring of Russians and the aboriginal population of Russian America or were natives who "pledged their political allegiance to the Tsar." (Oleksa; 1990; 185) In 1821 the creoles were granted a special social status equivalent to townsmen. (Fedorova; 1975; 13) "This allowed them" Fedorova writes, "to advance themselves on equal terms with Russians in government service and obtain officer's ranks." Between 1830 and 1840 creoles accounted for one quarter to one half of the Ross colony's population, and often outnumbered the Russians by as much as two to one. (Petrov; 1988; 64) One is tempted at this point to go straight to contemporary Russian costume sources and have a simple answer to what the majority of the colonists wore; unfortunately it is not so simple. V. Basanoff, writing in "The Archives of the Russian Church in Alaska" (*Pacific Historical Review*, Vol.II; 1933) states, "It is, however, characteristic of a new society that its social strata are not always determined by the class to which the newcomers belonged in the old country." Basanoff goes on to cite the case of Agafina Ivanova, a serf girl, the personal property of the nobleman A. G. Rotchev, who stood as godmother to several newly baptized children at Fort Ross. "Godparents usually belonged to a higher social strata, and in a small colony where everybody knew everybody we should consequently find in the rubric of spiritual parents only socially prominent people." This example alone would

SITKA INHABITANT
Jirokichi, 1842

not indicate that the inhabitants of Ross dressed in a manner that would indicate a higher social standing. Recalling E. Kuskova's example (see Part I, Administrators) and Zagoskin's remarks concerning dress and social status, a pattern seems to emerge. Zagoskin wrote in 1842 this description of creole women in the colonial capital, "With the spread of enlightenment came heightened luxury. Silk and lace dresses and satin bonnets were ordered from Petersburg for the creole girls and in these they used to go barefoot to fetch water." (1967; 68) The reference to the "spread of enlightenment" could refer to several things; the new privileges of 1821, the change in the administration of the colonies in 1818, or the arrival of Ioann Veniaminov and Baroness von Wrangell. Much had evidently changed since Baranov's time when the women "of honor" (undoubtedly natives) "though they did not abandon their parkas and still covered their faces with a sleeve when they encountered a man, began to make their parkas of Chinese satin brought in the ships of the North American states. This was the first step towards worldliness and luxury." This "heightened luxury" extended to even the smaller redoubt of St. Michael where Zagoskin wrote that the creole women "could all waltz skillfully, dance the French quadrille gracefully, all could knit scarves very well and little neckerchiefs and little caps." (1967; 258) These creoles were well aware of their social status and considered "any domestic occupation beneath her, as she firmly believes that because of her husband she should also be fed at company expense." (1967; 258) This "enlightenment" that brought creoles and natives into the Russian Empire as subjects also brought to them the customs and duties of colonial citizens. They were educated at company schools or sent to Russia for training. "To be creole came to mean that one had adopted certain Slavic European attitudes and traits, had been trained to some extent in a western type school, and thereby qualified for a position in the middle or upper management of the colony." (Oleksa; 1990; 188) As mentioned in Part I, these middle managers of the colonies were described as wearing clothing very similar to that of the townsmen and gentry of Russia. Illustrations from the journal of Jirokichi (Plummer; 1991) show the dresses and shirts typical of this class, and every other mention of creoles' dress confirms this conformity to European dress (Blaschke, Khlebnikov, Zagoskin, Veniaminov).

FEMININE STYLES
Jirokichi, 1842

Other than the drawings by Jirokichi, few pictures exist of creoles in Russian America. The illustration of rural Sitka in 1828 by von Kittlitz shows a woman in European dress similar to the illustration by Kozlinskii of a Russian townswoman of the first half of the nineteenth century. The text to Kozlinskii's illustration describes "A chemise of the Russian style made of white muslin, the skirt of ornamented silk material (satin or silk), the skirt sewn from a straight breadth of cloth tied on the top with a tape. The apron (from the style at the start of the century) is made of cambric, finished with a pleated gather and lace, the apron strings are made of colorful narrow ribbon, tied in a bow. Shoes, without heels, are made of colored Morocco leather. On the head is a muslin scarf adorned with golden flowers. Daily dress is sewn in the same manner, but using simpler cloth: chemise of linen, occasionally of calico, the skirt of colored linen, nankeen cloth, or blue fustian. The head scarf is simple apron linen. Women's or girls dresses are identical, the only difference is in the headdress; women entirely cover the hair, girls leave open the top and the braid.

RURAL SITKA
Friedrich H. von Kittlitz, 1828

TOWNSWOMAN
Ink Drawing
V. Kozlinskii

Men's fashion was closer to the European. Russians were very fond of a visored cap (*kartuz*) and occasionally wore their trousers inside their boots. (Malyshev, 1991) The type of cloth was often of a less expensive variety (frieze rather than broadcloth) for everyday use, and linen replaced cotton for office clothing. In 1991 the cemetery restoration project at Fort Ross unearthed a number of buttons with bits of black green frieze attached to and often surrounding the button. This was a rare chance to observe at close hand actual evidence of clothing at the Ross colony. The buttons, silver plated white metal or zinc, were attached to the cloth backing in a manner consistent with a uniform coat. The button holes, in black silk or linen showed a high quality of needlework equal to a professional tailor. Black green cloth had been prescribed by the company since 1805 as a suitable cloth for jackets and coats. The type of coat or jacket that these cloth fragments and buttons indicate would be very difficult to reconstruct, but it is, with so little evidence of clothing at this site, a tantalizing piece of a puzzle from which a picture of life at the fort is slowly beginning to form.

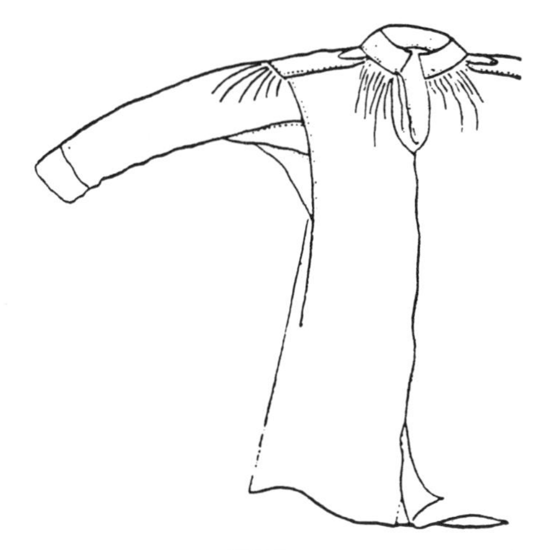

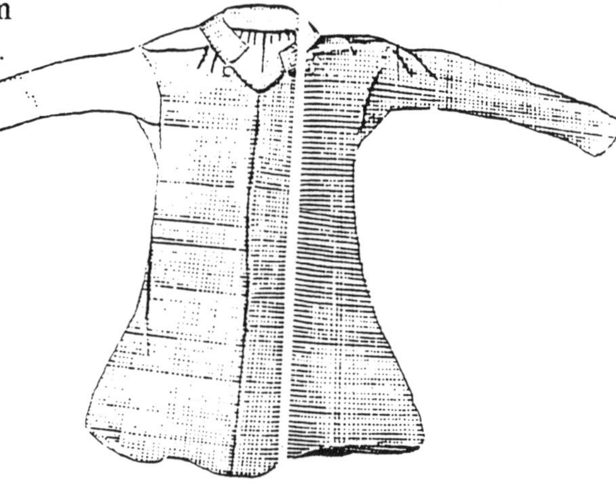

SITKA, ITEMS OF DAILY USE (MEN'S SHIRTS)
Jirokichi, 1842

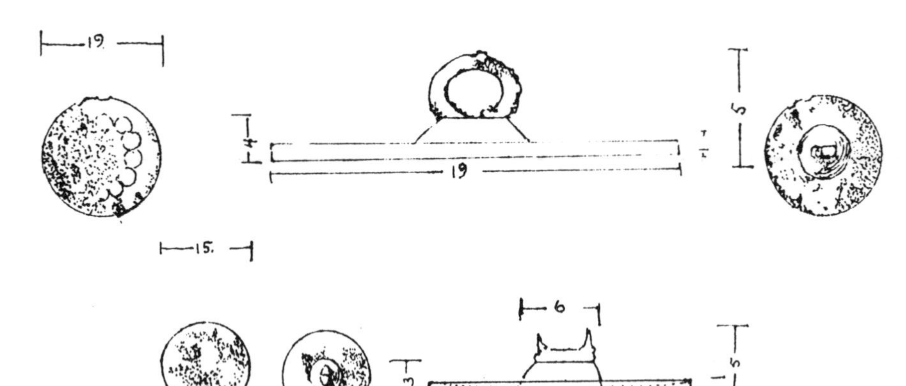

BUTTONS FROM CEMETERY RESTORATION
Ink Drawing, J. Middleton

PART III
LABORERS, NATIVE ALASKANS and NATIVE CALIFORNIANS

VIEW OF THE RUSSIAN CAPITAL (SITKA)
F. H. von Kittlitz, 1827

THE FORGE, L. Plakhov, 1845

PART III LABORERS

The working class at Colony Ross consisted not only of a social strata, but a multicultural group which was comprised of Russians (including various nationals within the European and Asian empire), Aleutian and Kodiak Islanders, California Indians, an occasional European, and at least one African. They were not only employees of the Russian-American Company, but in most cases indentured servitors in the worst possible sense. Before the emancipation of the serfs in Russia in 1861 men and women of the serf estate belonged either to the land or to their masters, and could be bought and sold, or simply rented out by their owners. The serfs who belonged to the land were, in the case of the Russian-American Company, "state serfs" whose services could be acquired by the company as long as the serf's taxes were paid to his home district. These serfs, predominantly from Siberia and northern Russia, were more enterprising and better suited the company's requirements. In 1820 the company specified particular kinds of employment for its applicants: "for construction of ships and buildings; for the felling of trees; for the making of fishing gear; for marine expeditions as well as for trapping animals; and for other duties; for fishing and for the preserving of fish; sailors; artillerymen; men to stand guard at the posts of the region; to work in the smithies and copper-foundries, or to do metal work; in other words to engage in all sorts of production. (Fedorova; 1975; 7) Peasants made up such a small percentage of the population, in what was principally a maritime trading operation, that by 1825 the company sought to obtain peasant-serfs for the Ross settlement, but was turned down by the government. "In 1822, the only Russian who knew how to farm, V. Antipin, had died" (Khlebnikov 199; 101). The peasant population continued to decline in Russian America in general, so that by 1855 there was "hardly anybody" who could carry on the necessary work. The state serfs who accepted employment in the company for California were, as noted above, more craftsmen than farmers. Most of those from northern Russia were at least partly literate (Malyshev, 1991), had traveled half way around the world, and in some cases knew foreign languages.

PACIFIC ISLANDER
Pavel Mikhailov, 1827, pencil

KILLING A GOAT
Jirokichi, 1842

The Russians who came to Fort Ross brought many traditional Russian aspects of their culture, but sadly there is no evidence as yet that they brought the richly decorated clothing of the Russian peasants. A clear lack of peasants may be the reason, or it may be that since the company was in the practice of issuing cloth for prescribed types of clothing, none of which describe peasant clothing, that the clothing of the colonists reflected a more European international look. Russian language resource material is more precise as concerns clothing descriptions than is English. The articles of dress which apply in particular to the peasant class, the *sarafan*, the *kosovarotka*, and other forms of *narodnaia odezhda* do not appear in the literature of Russian America. The single piece of circumstantial evidence, the ceremonial kamleika of the Aleuts, which is decorated in a way that would suggest the influence of the embroidered "kosovorotka" of northern Russia, or even the applique tunics of the Lapps, is described in Alaska only, and not recorded in California.

In 1805 the chief manager, A. A. Baranov, directed the company stores in the Ka'diak and Unalaska districts to have available the following materials for the production of clothing for employees: a coat of frieze or soldier's cloth; two jackets of soldier's cloth, one for dress occasions; three pairs of trousers, made of soldier's cloth, one for dress occasions, other trousers made of linen, chamois, and perhaps nankeen or drill; shirts of "alexandrine striped linen, blue suzdal, blue Chinese cotton", and perhaps nankeen or drill; drawers of unbleached linen; unbleached linen linings which might be added to coats and jackets; a chamois waistcoat and kamleika." (Pierce; 1976; 189-190, 230) The above materials, with some slight exceptions, are very similar to the type of clothing issued to Russian naval sailors during the first half of the nineteenth century. The Russian word used for jacket "kurtka" in this particular instance, was also used at that time to identify the naval sailor's jacket. Given that these articles were to be made of "soldier's cloth" it would be reasonable to assume that these were quite similar in appearance.

In 1836 Richard Henry Dana visited a Russian-American ship anchored in San Francisco Bay. Describing the crew, he noted, "They had, every one of them, double soled boots, coming up to the knees, and well greased, thick woolen trousers, frocks, waistcoats, pea jackets, woolen caps..." (Dana; 1946; 249) This outfit, as described by Dana, closely

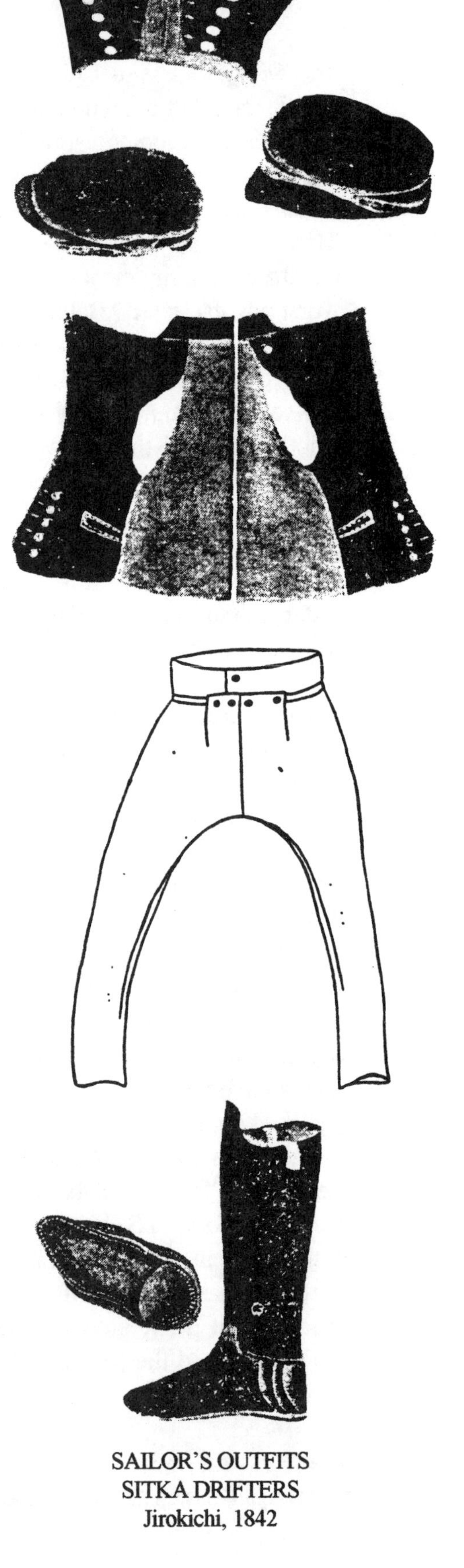

SAILOR'S OUTFITS
SITKA DRIFTERS
Jirokichi, 1842

resembles the uniform of the Imperial Navy. Although the implication would be that the employees of the Russian-American Company in California wore clothing that resembled a military uniform, two eye witness accounts, at least, in Russian-America state that there was no uniform appearance (Golovnin; 1979, Belcher; 1979: 58). The availability of military cloth in the company's stores, uniforms or cloth supplied to both Sutter and Vallejo, and the remains of uniform frieze from the recent cemetery restoration project at Fort Ross confirms its use here. In 1842 the Japanese drifter Jirokichi illustrated his companions in clothing issued to them in Sitka. The short jackets, fall front trousers, and visored caps are clearly those of sailors. Two Pacific Islanders drawn by Pavel Mikhailov in 1827 show one wearing a very common European style shirt and the other wearing the enlisted man's coat typical of the Russian Navy. Before 1840 in most navies the enlisted crew wore non uniform but distinctly seaman's clothing. The Russian navy appeared to be the exception, uniforming its crews earlier than other navies. The typical dress of the merchant seaman would seem to be very much like the navy, for in the early 1850's when the first regulations appear for various shipping companies, the uniforms are almost identical, but without the rank distinctions (*Polnoe sobranie zakonov*; 1851).

DRIFTERS IN SAILOR'S OUTFITS, Jirokichi, 1842

The cloth available to the colonists would suggest that a great deal more variety was to be had than that for the average seaman. In addition to the military frieze and linen linings there were English bombazines, Chinese cottons, Flemish linens and English woolens. An employee could easily go into debt to outfit himself and his family with even the most basic cloth, let alone the satins and fine cloth available at the Ross store (von Wrangel; 1834; no. 61) By the 1830's much had changed from the rougher, more self-sufficient times in the Alaska of 1805, and employees at Ross had more to choose from in their store. Communications between the colonial capitol and its California settlement were greatly improved. By 1825 both the quality and quantity of goods shipped to Ross indicated an improvement in the material life of its inhabitants.

PACIFIC ISLANDER
Pavel Mikhailov, 1827, pencil

Aleutian and Kodiak Islanders in the employ of the company were in much the same position as their Russian serf counterparts. "They were virtual slaves of the Russian-

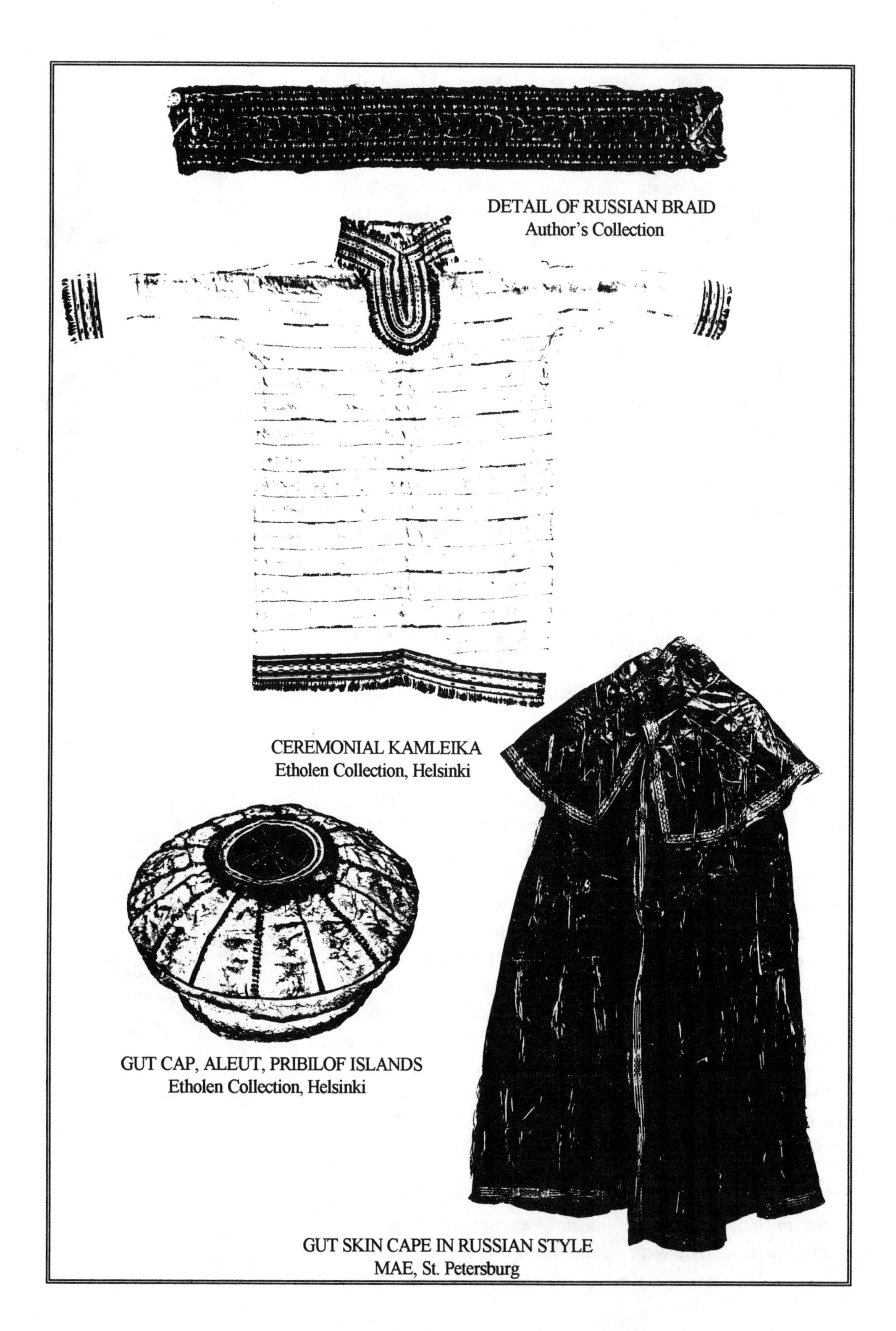

DETAIL OF RUSSIAN BRAID
Author's Collection

CEREMONIAL KAMLEIKA
Etholen Collection, Helsinki

GUT CAP, ALEUT, PRIBILOF ISLANDS
Etholen Collection, Helsinki

GUT SKIN CAPE IN RUSSIAN STYLE
MAE, St. Petersburg

American Company, their lives controlled by the Russian managers." (Veltre; 1990; 177) There is much more evidence of the Aleuts adopting the dress of their masters than the Russians incorporating native dress as their own. Some pieces of Aleut dress better suited to the local conditions were indeed adopted, and in many cases culturally intermingled to produce a garment that was a product of both. (Ray; 1981) The well known gut parka (kamleika) as mentioned before, may have been decorated with an Aleut version of Russian metal braid or embroidery. The cape worn by sea captains was an adaptation of a European cape coat (Black; 1988; 79) Gut cap covers were produced to rainproof the Russian caps. (Varjola; 1990; 182) Kamleikas were issued to the hunters as part of their outfits, often at company expense. The kamleika proved very popular with the Russians too. In 1816 Otto von Kotzebue outfitted his crew with two kamleikas for each crew member. (Black; 1982; 157)

Beginning in Baranov's time the Aleut women began to abandon their skin parkas in favor of cloth ones. In 1832 Khlebnikov wrote "on Sitka they want to have clothes made not of regular soldier's cloth, but from good frieze or fine wool. Many of them wear frock coats and dress coats. Their wives were formerly delighted to have parkas of rodent fur and cotton kamleikas, but here they all want a printed çotton dress, a shawl, etc. (1976; 105) Father Veniaminov, in the colonies at the same time, wrote, "Many Aleuts can be seen in frieze or cloth jackets and even frock coats, (however the latter are only for the toyons and eminent ones). At present many of them wear boots, and the women shoes. Shirts were not entirely unknown to the Aleuts in former times but are now in general use. The Aleuts even wear waistcoats, trousers (which formerly also were unknown), and neckties (cravats); and the women and daughters dress for holidays in [stylish Russian dress and shawls]." (Fedorova; 1973; 229 [Dr. Serov's translation])

SITKA INHABITANTS
Jirokichi, 1842

Lt. Zagoskin, writing a few years later in 1842, noted that in the "more important settlements, the Aleuts go about in jackets and frock coats, their wives and daughters in calico dresses and kamleika, which are long shirts made of ticking or nankeen with red cloth (wool military broad cloth) trimming around the collar and hem. The married women, guarding against sin, keep their heads always covered while the girls wear their hair long, tied at the back of the neck with a ribbon." (1956; 87) Pavel Mikhailov, in Alaska in 1827 made a drawing of young girls picking berries in shirts which closely correspond to those in Zagoskin's description. "Concerning ticking. . . The Aleuts especially like these materials. They are also used by the Kenais and Aglegmiuts, who make women's kamleiki out of them. . ." (Khlebnikov; 94; 203) The similarity of these fashions to those of young girls in northern Russia is striking and is very close indeed to the shirts worn by the Russian serf class. The cloths worn like shawls in the drawing also imitates the Russian townsman fashion.

SUNDAY ON UNALASKA
I. G. Voznesenskii, 1843

Von Kittlitz also wrote concerning the working outfits of the Aleuts "Likewise the highly original head adornment as well as the national costume was disappearing more and more and being gradually replaced by Russian clothing." (Litke; 1987; 183) Two of Voznesenskii's drawings illustrate this Russian influence in 1843. "Sunday on Unalaska" and "Cape Espenberg, Kotzebue Sound" show Aleuts in Russian visored caps and kamleikas. It is likely that Russian clothing is being worn beneath the kamleikas.

The clothing most described for this period in Russian America is everyday clothing or what would be described in the military as service dress. Except for the kamleikas, working dress is seldom mentioned. The lists of cloth and clothing available to the workers, and the type of outfits suggested by the administration would seem to follow fairly closely to the typical working class outfits of Russia and Europe of the period. A long smock or work shirt of linen or "doba", a blue heavy linen or cotton similar to sail cloth, worn outside the trousers was quite common for workers and sailors at this time (and even continued in use up until the second half of this century), and trousers tucked into calf length or high boots for work was common to many European nations. The laborers at Colony Ross are described as making their trousers from soft deer suede (Khlebnikov; 1988; 59). This style was later adopted by the Russian army in the Caucasian War, and the soldiers became known for their red brown suede trousers.

CAPE ESPENBERG
KOTZEBUE SOUND
I.G. Voznesenskii, 1843

INHABITANTS OF UNALASKA, F. H. von Kittlitz, 1828

The elegant hat worn by the two hunters is part of the old national costume of the Aleuts and becomes from day to day more rare among them. It is made of wood which, by being soaked, is changed to a ductile material, like papier mache. Its ornaments consist of chiseled bone, work in which the Aleuts excel, as well as chips of glass and sea lion whiskers on which they thread more chips and which make the head look more like that of this animal. In the distance can be seen a a two-hatch canoe; the structure of which differs little from the one-hatch canoes which are the most used. F. H von Kittlitz

YOUNG GIRLS, Pavel Mikhailov, 1827, pencil

This picture might be a new corrected edition of that which La Perouse included in his atlas, under the title of "Women of Port-des-Francais". It should give a more favorable idea of the women of this country, who in our days have decidedly a less savage air, since they abandoned their skin garments and adopted more polite manners. But this sketch has failed almost completely, since all the figures have undergone serious alterations. The cheeks are too hollow, because in reality the faces of the women of the island are as round as a full moon. They have a certain harmony in their expressions, although they are rarely free of a sullen look, especially about the lips, which anyway is not surprising in people who are still so coarse. Their national beauty consists principally on their big dark eyes whose expression is generally sweet and animated. F. H. von Kittlitz

CALIFORNIA INDIANS TELLING FORTUNES
L. Choris

Concerning ticking. The promyshlenniks and Koloshes in general use ticking to make their shirts. The type they need are made of inexpensive linen. They rarely use half-cotton or full cotton cloth because of their cost. Ticks and deburets are used to make hospital robes, sheets and light work clothes. The Aleuts especially like these materials. . . . in California this material is in general use by the Indians because of its durability and is readily bought at the mission by the Indians. (Khlebnikov; 94; 203)

The closest image, in this case hunters in Kamchatka in 1826 was drawn by von Kittlitz on the Litke expedition. The man on the right wears the common European-style shirt and either breeches or trousers tucked into boots (unclear) while the man on the left wears the typical serf costume of northern Russia. The sheepskin coat and red wool cap trimmed with fur appear often in depictions of serfs in the first quarter of the nineteenth century.

HUNTERS, KAMCHATKA
F. H. von Kittlitz, 1827

The Indian inhabitants of the Ross colony were described as early as 1818 by the officers and expedition artist of the Russian naval sloop of war "Kamchatka". F. P. Litke wrote that the Indians "walk around completely naked, although some of them have blankets from the Spaniards and Russians which they remake into some sort of shirt." (Safaralieva 1991; 1) Litke also described other articles of attire; a short cloak made of seagull skin, and women wearing "sheepskin" tied around their waist, hanging below the knee. Mikhail Tikhanov, the expedition's artist sent by the Academy of Fine Arts, St. Petersburg, made a watercolor of this dress. F. F. Matiushkin, another officer on board noted in his diary two incidents which corroborate Tikhanov's views of the Indians. "Born in pleasant and moderate climate, they walk completely naked, while women cover themselves with the fur of coyotes." (Safaralieva 1991; 2)

The administrator of Fort Ross, Peter Kostromitinov, writing in the 1830's noted little had changed in the preceding ten or more years, and the Indians still preferred nakedness. The clothing which was provided by the Russians was not worn in conformity to Russian standards, and men were seen wearing women's dresses or several shirts worn all at once. "In contacts with Russians, Indians must have been dressed at least with the minimum, because Russian etiquette considered nakedness as indecent." (Safaralieva 1991; 2)

INHABITANT OF RUMIANTSEV BAY
Mikhail T. Tikhanov, 1818, watercolor

PART IV
NAVY AND MERCHANT SHIPPERS

ALGARUM VEGETATIO
A. F. Postels, 1827

NAVY AND MERCHANT SHIPPERS

In 1817 the navy, alarmed at reports of abuses among the employees of the Russian-American Company concerning the native population of the colonies, and corruption among the administrators, convinced the Russian government and the directors of the company in St. Petersburg that the administration of Russian America belonged in the more capable hands of their officers. Many of the concerns expressed by the navy were found later to be groundless. The change had already been effected, however, and all subsequent governors of the colonies were naval officers in company service.

F. P. VON WRANGELL

Naval administration did little to change the appearance of colonial life until the middle of the 19th century. In 1851 a uniform was introduced for officers serving on the company's ships, and soldiers from Siberian regiments were sent to Alaska to serve as sentries. During the years of the Ross colony, the only uniform which would have been seen (except for the civil service uniform) would have been that of the officers and sailors of the Imperial Russian Navy.

The naval ships which called in the ports of California in the first half of the 19th century were predominantly those of the Baltic fleet, based in Kronstadt. The Imperial Navy had two fleets, the Baltic, and the Black Sea Fleet, based in Sevastopol. There was also a Pacific squadron, but it was made up of the ships of the Baltic Fleet, and the ships rotated back to Kronstadt or Sveaborg when finished with their station.

O. E. KOTZEBUE

The Baltic Fleet used the numerous round-the-world voyages in the first half of the 19th century to train its officers and men in the blue water seamanship it required to become a world class naval power. Many of the junior officers who came to California on ships such as the *Riurik, Kamchatka, Kreiser,* and *Apollon* later entered company service and became administrators, and in many cases governors. There were, among these young officers, future naval heroes such as Admiral Nakhimov and Prince Maksutov, Governors Etholen, von Wrangell and Teben'kov, and others such as Lisianskii, Davydov, Kotzebue, Lazarev, and Zavalishin, famous in Russian naval history. This ocean training was all the more valuable for the sailors of the Baltic.

"The Baltic Fleet spent six months or more of each year in dry dock. The men spent most of their time perfecting the marching skills considered more important than seamanship. By contrast, under the inspired leadership of Admiral Lazarev, and later Admirals Kornilov and Nakhimov, the Black Sea Fleet spent most of its time perfecting nautical skills." (Thomas; 1991; 11)

M. P. LAZAREV

The Russian sailor during the reign of Nikolai I had much more in common with soldiers than with sailors of other countries. Uniformed much earlier than other navies, Russian sailors were expected to be seagoing soldiers and perform the duties of both. The navy was organized into units called "ekipazhes" which contained 1,000 sailors, 80 noncomissioned officers, 30 officers and 25 buglers and drummers. The ekipazh was divided into four companies, and these companies supplied the crews required to man the ships of the fleet. "A ship's crew also contained an unspecified number of naval artillery, navigators and engineer officers, and men of the labor ekipazhi who furnished sailmakers, caulkers and carpenters. The addition of these men allowed an ekipazh to be dispersed among several ships." (Thomas; 1991; 12)

Sailors often appear in the records of Fort Ross. Some were left from ships like the *Riurik* to assist with the colony's first shipbuilding efforts. Others, like the sailors from the *Kreiser*, Iakov Statin and Petr Grigor'ev, may have found life in California irresistible and jumped ship. They were returned and put to work on the *Kiakhta* as seamen, and later returned to Sitka aboard the *Baikal.*

ALGARUM VEGETATIO
(detail) A. F. Postels, 1827

There are frequent examples of sailor's uniforms in the works of the artists aboard the Russian round-the-world voyages of 1827 and 1829. A. F. Postels in his drawing 'Algarum Vegetatio" shows a sailor assisting a naturalist gathering specimens in what may be the environs of Sitka sound. The sailor is wearing the "walking out dress" for summer: the black "kurtka" (sailor's jacket) and the black, piped in white "bezkozirka" (visorless cap introduced in 1811). White linen or cotton trousers were worn in summer, black wool in winter. Pavel Mikhailov shows the same uniform being worn by sailors in the South Pacific "*Men of Vostok and Mirnyi in New Zealand*" 1820, and another drawing shows the oarsmen

SAILORS AT A BOOTMAKERS
A. Denisov, 1832

of the captain's gig wearing shirts with their black silk ties and duty caps, while the officers, in contrast, wore the dress uniform of coatee and, in the captain's case, black wool trousers (in the tropics!) The crews, occupied in physical labor, have obviously been given permission to remove their jackets and row in comfort.

A sailor was expected to have in his sea chest a parade uniform consisting of a jacket, white or black trousers, a shako, and dress boots; a duty uniform with jacket, white or black trousers, cap, and calf length boots; a work uniform made of sailcloth or blue cloth, cap and work boots; a winter uniform of a greatcoat, and for standing watch in heavy snow, a fur lined leather coat. The latter was issued only by the watch officer, and only a few were kept by each company. "Sailors at a Bootmakers" by A. Denisov, 1832, illustrates very nicely both the duty uniform (right) and the working rig of the 1830's sailor. Each sailor had three kurtkas. The best was used for parades, second best for everyday duty, and the one in poorest condition was used for working duty aboard ship or in barracks. For hard labor, the "roba", or sailcloth work uniform was employed. When at last the kurtka was worn out, it was cut apart and used for patches or to make caps, the cloth being turned inside out to make replacement cuffs, collars, or sleeves. (Viktor Malyshev; 1991)

MEN OF VOSTOK AND MIRNYI IN NEW ZEALAND
Pavel Mikhailov, 1820

Rank distinction among the noncommissioned officers was evidenced by a wide strip of metallic braid worn around the collar and cuffs, and a narrower strip of braid worn on the shoulder strap for junior noncommissioned officers, and the wider type for the senior noncommissioned officers. Long service chevrons were worn on the left arm. The Guard's Ekipazh of the Imperial Guard, stationed in St. Petersburg, wore the same uniform as the Fleet, with some distinctions. Their buttons bore the Imperial eagle with crossed anchors, in contrast to the single anchor of the Fleet. The shoulder straps for the Guards were red rather than the black or white straps of the Fleet, and the leather cross straps for the cartridge pouch and sword, which were black for the Fleet, were white for the Guards. Sailors of the Guard's Ekipazh were distributed among the ships of the Baltic Fleet and in times of war, were comparable to the marines of other countries.

Pavel Mikhailov, 1820

Officers used several different uniforms and, in addition, variations on these. The parade uniform was a black coatee with black or white trousers, epaulets, cocked hat and sword. A naval dagger (kortik) could also be worn, and a visored cap with cockade (after 1835) could substitute for the cocked hat and sword. With the parade uniform medals and orders were always worn. The duty dress for officers was the frock coat, worn with cap and kortik, or an officer's jacket (here in summer) as illustrated by Karl Briullov in 1836. A white cap cover is worn over the officer's cap, and black pumps are worn with the white narrow fall trousers. There was, in addition, an officer's grey cape coat with black collar worn in winter. There were uniform changes in 1835 and 1837 which concerned the navy, but aside from the establishment of a single breasted parade uniform (as illustrated in the Etholin portrait) they concerned mostly details in the epaulet and the establishment of the cockade for officer's caps. The epaulets for the navy identified the wearer's rank and to which ekipazh the officer belonged. Epaulets without fringe identified a junior officer below kapitan, lieutenant, and the numeral identified to which ekipazh the wearer belonged. In the 1840's the black background color was changed to metallic braid and the numbers discarded. The system of rank stars remained.

CAPTAIN-LIEUTENANT
V. A. KORNILOV
Karl Briullov, 1836

The officers of the Russian-American Company prior to 1851 had no uniform. "Officers of the fleet, going into service with the Russian-American Company, were dismissed from military service with the right to wear the uniform, retain the rank and symbols of the navy fleet officer." (Belik; 1992; 2) V. M. Golovnin in 1817 tried to clarify the difference between the Russian-American Company's commercial vessels and the Imperial Navy's warships to the Spanish Viceroy in Peru. "I had to explain that there is a great difference between Russian warships and trading vessels, even though the trade ships which had been in port were also under the command of officers of the Imperial Fleet who wore uniforms just like those on our ship." (Golovnin; 1979; 67)

M. N. VASIL'EV

Sailors employed by the company are mentioned in the previous chapter as wearing clothing very similar to that of the navy, though there is no evidence that any uniform appearance was attempted. When Richard Henry Dana continued his description of the crew of the Russian brig anchored in Yerba Buena in 1836 he wrote, "The clothing of one of these men would weigh nearly as much as that of half our crew. They had brutish faces, looked like the antipodes of sailors, and apparently dealt in nothing but grease. They lived upon grease; ate it, drank it, slept in the midst of it, and their clothes were covered with it." Dana alludes to the difference between naval and merchant sailors when he describes the ship itself, "The top masts, top gallant masts, and studding booms were nearly black for want of scraping, and the decks would have turned the stomach of a man-of-war's man." (Dana; 1946; 250) Russian naval officers had a different view of their company's ships. Lieutenant Zavoiko writing in 1835-1838 in Novo Arkhangel'sk noted that, "Vessels of our company, which in their cleanliness and handsomeness cede nothing to either English or American naval vessels in all anchorages where, when assembled with them, merited our entire attention. (Polevoi; 1994; 349)

V. M. GOLOVNIN

Fleet Captain Lieutenant F. Litke, writing in the 1830's from his notes made on the round-the-world voyage on the *Seniavin,* addressed the problem of military discipline in the Company. "The severity of military discipline is indispensable here in order to keep not only the Americans in check, but also the promyshlenniks themselves, among whom it would be well nigh impossible not to find some unruly and vicious natured men; these however, are carefully surveyed. The carrying out of orders, the receipt of reports, the guards, the patrols, reveille, the retreat - all the duties are carried out in detail here according to regulations and with a certain solemnity. Naval officers are always in uniform" (1987; 53) It would be interesting to know if the captain of the Russian brig in Yerba Buena was a company official or a foreign captain contracted to officer a company ship.

A. A. ETHOLEN

APPENDICES

ПОДЪ ВЫСОЧ. ЕГО ИМП: ВЕЛИЧ: ПОКРОВИТ:
РОССИС. АМЕРИ
КАНС. КОМПА
НИЙ ПЕЧАТЬ

ILLUSTRATIONS

The illustrations in this book are, whenever possible, taken from original drawings and paintings of the 1830s and 1840s. Those painted by the artists N. A. Bestuzhev and N. P. Repin are a particularly valuable resource because they illustrate clothing worn in Siberia in an institutional setting between 1825 and 1840. Individuals pictured are members of the gentry of urban Russia exiled to Siberia for their participation in the Decembrist movement. Given the "institutional" nature of prison life, the type of dress worn by these exiles would likely have been worn in the farthest reaches of the colonial Russian Empire. Future Decembrists actually visited Fort Ross. "The Russian colonies in America apparently were often discussed by the members of the Northern Society. Russian America, and in part Fort Ross, occupied a special place in the Decembrists' plans." Khlebnikov; 1994; xxviii [Fedorova's commentary])

DECEMBRIST SETTLEMENT IN SIBERIA, N. A. Bestuzhev

ILLUSTRATIONS OF ADMINISTRATORS

DECEMBRISTS AT THE GATE OF FORT CHITA IN WINTER, 1828-1830, N.P. Repin

RECONSTRUCTION

(Illustration by Viktor N. Malyshev)

The central figure wears the frock coat and cap of the Russian civil service uniform. The coat was made of black green frieze or wool broadcloth, as was the cap. The buttons, either brass gilt or silver colored, usually bore the design of the ministry or provincial government to which the official was attached. As no button design was approved for the Company until 1851, it was likely plain or with a civil design (see button from the Fort Ross cemetery). The cap visor was black lacquered leather, and the black green or white trousers (pantaloons) bore a leather strap which went below the boots.

The figure on the left wears townsman or merchant clothing. This would be typical of the dress of the middle managers of the colonies. The cloth was typically soldiers' (black green frieze) and the shirt, here the kosovorotka, could be made of a fine linen, nankeen, or a fine checked cloth called pestriadi. Blue twill cotton for work was also popular. The cap (kartuz) could have a cloth or black lacquered leather visor. Boots with the trousers tucked in were worn for work.

The worker on the right wears the hat popular in northern Russia, and is made of stiff light brown or grey wool felt. The mottled look of the fabric would indicate a pestriadi for the shirt, and a striped linen with design, for the trousers. Aprons were often a very heavy natural colored linen.

Concerning broadcloth. During Mr. Baranov's management of the colonies, frieze was generally used to make clothing; soon after it was replaced by linen; good soldier's linen and the ordinary type of linen are comfortable for worker's clothing. (Khlebnikov; 94; 204)

PORTRAIT OF A MERCHANT IN PROVINCIAL MERCHANT UNIFORM
Kalashnikov, 1840s

RECONSTRUCTION

Civil servants' uniforms of the 1830s. The coatee is made of dark green wool broadcloth; the trousers or breeches of fine white linen. Black shoes were worn. The cocked hat, here a bicorn, was made of black felt, with a black silk ribbon trim and gold lace. One can note the similar button and pocket arrangement with the coatee illustrated above (and with the frock coat back view). The frock coat on the right was of similar material, and worn with white or black green trousers. Court style swords were worn with these uniforms, as in the Kuskov portrait. Either of these coats could be pictured in the portrait. Decorations were not usually worn with the frock coat, except those worn at the neck or in the buttonhole. The gold lace on the collar and cuff indicated the rank of the wearer.

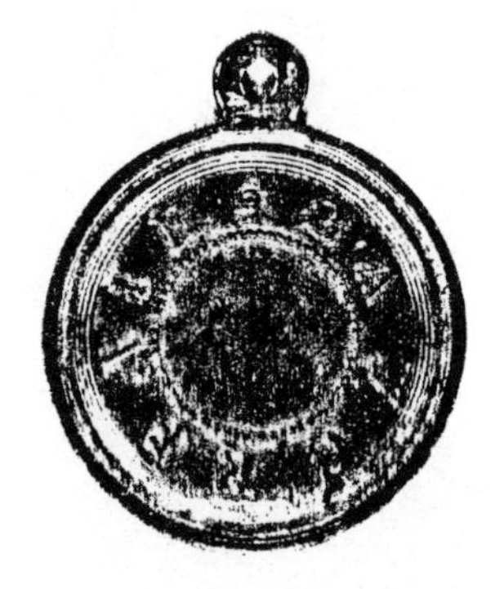

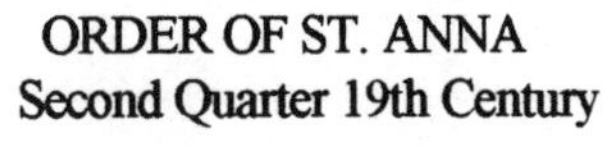

ORDER OF ST. ANNA
Second Quarter 19th Century

COURT SWORD
Late 18th Century

MEDAL FOR ZEALOUS SERVICE
Nikolai I Period

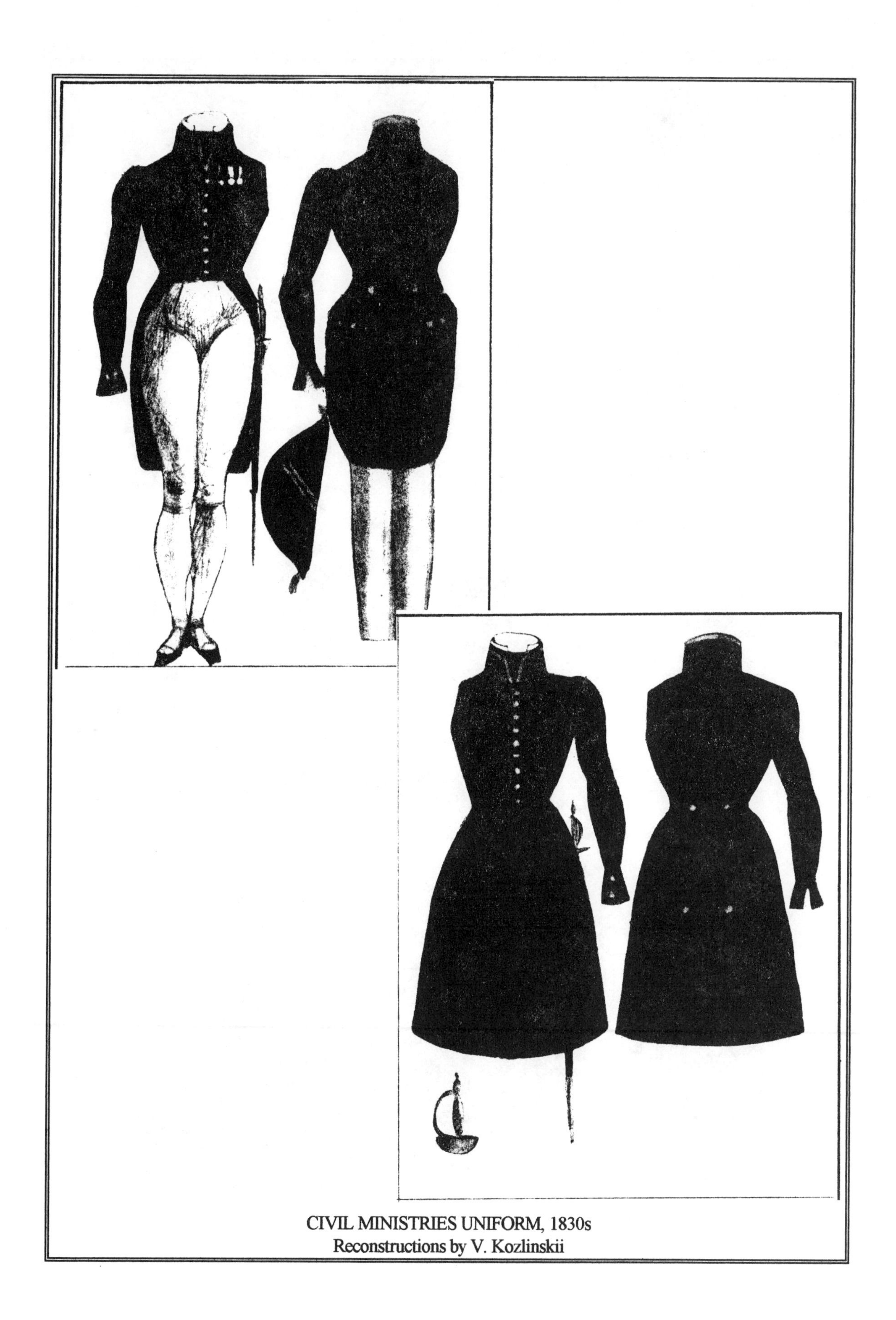

CIVIL MINISTRIES UNIFORM, 1830s
Reconstructions by V. Kozlinskii

DECEMBRIST GENTLEMEN 1830s - 1840s, N. P. Repin

DECEMBRIST GENTLEMEN 1830s - 1840s, N. A. Bestuzhev

DECEMBRIST GENTLEMEN 1830s - 1840s, N. A. Bestuzhev

DECEMBRIST GENTLEMEN 1830s - 1840s, N. A. Bestuzhev

DECEMBRIST GENTLEMEN 1830s - 1840s, N. A. Bestuzhev

DECEMBRIST GENTLEMEN 1830s - 1840s, N. A. Bestuzhev

DECEMBRIST GENTLEMEN 1830s - 1840s, N. A. Bestuzhev

DECEMBRIST LADIES 1830s - 1840s, (various artists)

DECEMBRIST LADIES 1830s - 1840s, (various artists)

PORTRAIT OF P. A. SPASSKII, 1829, N. D. Myl'nikov

PORTRAIT OF A MERCHANT'S WIFE, 1830s, artist unknown

PORTRAIT OFA MERCHANT'S WIFE A. B. DVORNIKOV, 1829, N. T. Durnov

Evgraf Krendovskii, *PORTRAIT OF THE ARTIST'S DAUGHTERS* (above)
A. Venetsianov, *PORTRAIT NASTEN'KA KHAVSHAIA*, 1826

A. Venetsianov, *PORTRAIT OF PANAEV CHILDREN*, 1841 (above left)
Grigory Soroka, *STUDY IN THE HOUSE AT OSTROVSKII*, 1844 (above right)
Yevgraf Krendovsky, *PORTRAIT OF SENATOR A. BASHILOV AND THE CHILDREN OF COUNT DE BALMAINE* (below)

DECEMBRIST CHILDREN 1830s -1840s, A. Maniani

Kuchikov, *PORTRAIT OF THE MERCHANT FAMILY KOSINIKH AT TEA*, 1840s

TOWNSMAN AND WOMAN, ink drawing reconstruction , V. Kozlinskii

ILLUSTRATIONS OF TOWNSMEN AND CREOLE CLOTHING

TOWNSPEOPLE IN THE FOREST, 1840, A. Shchokin (above)

RECONSTRUCTION
(Illustration by John Middleton)

A townsman in work clothing. The hat is a spruce-root hat made by Native Alaskans and sold by the Company in the colonies. These hats were sometimes painted with designs to produce a colorful effect. The silk tie is worn loosely around the opened collar shirt. The suspenders typical of Russian style of that time, are buttoned to narrow-fall trousers made of linen or soldier's cloth. The very soft leather boots had rather thin soles and low heels for urban wear, and had thicker or doubled soles and higher heels for the country or for work.

About friezes, flannelettes and flannels. Part of the frieze cloth is designated for trade with the Kolosh; the rest, along with the flannelette and flannel, is used for winter clothing for the families of officials and workers. (Khlebnikov; 94; 204)

PAINTED SRUCE ROOT HAT, TLINGIT
Etholen Collection, Helsinki

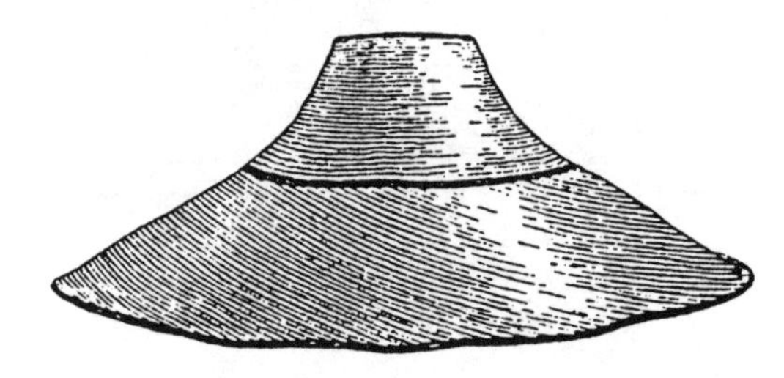

19TH CENTURY SPRUCE ROOT HATS COLLETED BY RUSSIANS, MAE collection

RECONSTRUCTION
(Illustration by John Middleton)

A creole in office clothing. The outfit is similar to European fashion of the same time. Popular cloth for this period and location were black-green, brown, olive, blue and tan. A different colored waistcoat was often worn, and trousers were often of a lighter color than the frock coat. The cloth cap or *kartuz* had either a visor of the same material, or a black lacquered leather one.

Concerning woolen cloth. The dark-green is designated for use by the officials; the red by the Aleuts who use the threads to embellish their kamleika, parkas and baidarkas, etc. (Khlebnikov; 94; 204)

MAN'S WOOLEN VEST, 1840s

RECONSTRUCTION

(Illustration by John Middleton)

A woman of the townsman class. A straw hat is worn over the mob cap, and secured with fine silk colored ribbons. A wool or silk shawl is worn around the neck and shoulders, and pinned in front. The dress is made from imported print fabric, often from India or China. In colder weather, a bonnet or cap with scarf would be worn, and the weight of the material would be greater, and undergarments increased. Leather ankle books or slippers were worn.

Concerning coarse calico. Thin calicos are designated for the officials, while the grey American calico is used mainly in Sitkha for trade with the Kolosh, who are paid in calico for small fur pelts; to a certain extent, by established custom, this material has now become a barter good. The Kolosh who sell bear skins of various sizes, price them as 2, 3 and 4 sazhens of calico or at 5, 7 1/2 and 10 arshins. With the calico we buy sheep and other goods from them. (Khlebnikov, 94; 203)

KERCHIEFS, MOSCOW PROVINCE
Late 18th - Early 19th Centuries

RECONSTRUCTION

(Illustration by John Middleton)

The everyday dress of the townswoman inside the house. A simple blouse, in the Russian style, was worn with a shawl, often in a plaid or print design. For outdoors, married women would cover the cap and all hair with a scarf, unmarried women showing braids or the hair on the forehead. The skirt, often in nankeen cotton or linen was gathered at the waist with a narrow band and tied with a piece of tape. The shoes were a soft, often colored leather, with low heels. A townswoman would also wear a stiffened cap beneath the scarf resembling the serf class "kokoshnik". A simple linen or printed cotton apron was also in common use, although not illustrated here.

Nankeen. The colonies prefer getting Cantonese nankeen because it is larger in size, and one piece of it is sufficient to make someone a coat or dress, and the price is almost the same as that of calico. When there is no means of getting Cantonese calico, we can get Kiakhta nankeen, which is cherry-colored, glossy and non-glossy, and has great breadth. The Russian nankeen brought here on the ship Elena was of good quality, but it faded quickly, and could only be sold when needed. If the color of the cloth becomes more durable and does not fade, it may replace the Cantonese and Kiakhta nankeen. This would be more advantageous because it is cheaper. (Khlebnikov; 94; 202)

SHAWL (DETAIL), 1840s
Guchkov Factory, Moscow

TOWNSMAN'S COAT, Ink drawing reconstruction by V.Kozlinskii

DUNIA, THE STATIONMASTER'S DAUGHTER
(PORTRAIT OF RUSSIAN TOWNSWOMAN), First Half of the 19th Century

KITCHEN (PAINTING OF RUSSIAN TOWNSWOMAN, DETAIL) Gurii Krylov, 1826-27

TOWNSWOMEN

THE LACEMAKER, V. A. Tropinin, 1823 (above), *LACEMAKING*, V. A. Tropinin, 1830

TOWNSWOMAN
GIRL WITH A POT OF ROSES, V. A. Tropinin, 1850

GIRL WITH A DOG, V. A. Tropinin, 1820s-1830s (above)
GIRL WEARING A SHAWL, A. Venetsianov, 1830

BOY RELEASING A GOLDFINCH, V. A. Tropinin, 1825 (above)
GIRL WITH A DOLL, V. A. Tropinin, 1841

ILLUSTRATIONS OF LABORERS

VIEW OF RURAL SITKA, F. H. von Kittlitz, 1828

This picture, not very important in itself, shows a habitation outside the town of Novo-Arkhangel'sk.... All the individuals that one sees in the foreground are the inhabitants of the colony; those seen farther away are the aborigines of the country. Unfortunately, the national characteristics of these small figures are missing from the engraving, and changes have been made. Now it will be impossible to make up for this by notes or explanations. Nevertheless, we believe we must point out the narrow bodice and the large petticoat such as one sees here, are entirely foreign to the costume of the women of Sitka. F. H. von Kittlitz

RECONSTRUCTION
(Illustration by Viktor N. Malyshev)

The figure on the left wears the frock coat cut in a manner somewhat out of date and decidedly provincial. The haircut and beard and the pants tucked into high leather boots identify him as a **merchant**. The merchant class had three levels with different rights and status. The highest grade were the urban merchants, who dressed with little distinction from the gentry. The provincial merchants often retained the customs and elements of dress of the rural peasants (haircut, beard and boots) while incorporating such status symbols as the frock coat and often the top hat.

The Company employee (promyshlennik) wears the cloth cap typical of the 1830s and the rural serf's frieze coat with a woven sash as belt. The trousers, of striped linen are also typical of the rural serf. A leather or cloth strap worn across the shoulder supports a cartridge pouch. The musket is the Tula military model.

Concerning ticking. The promyshlenniks and Koloshes in general use ticking to make their shirts. The type they need are made of inexpensive linen. They rarely use half-cotton or full cotton cloth because of their cost. (Khlebnikov; 94; 203)

PORTRAIT OF MERCHANT, V. D'iakonov, 1836

RECONSTRUCTION

(Illustration by John Middleton)

The Aleut employee in the working clothes of the 1830s. a forage cap is worn here, and may have been covered with a gut skin cover to waterproof it. Different color combinations were popular, and most seem to have been military surplus. The figure here wears beneath the gut skin kamleika, the "roba", or sailor's linen work shirt. The standing collar has been folded down. The boots are soft soled Siberian and Central Asian type, and have no heels. They were usually made from sea or land mammal hides.

Flemish linen. In Sitkha it is used to make tents for workers who work in the forests; it is used as a trade item with the Kolosh and to make light summer sailor's clothing; part of it is sold in California. This linen is used by the various offices to mainly make sails for baidaras, tents, clothing for workers and Aleuts. (Khlebnikov; 94; 204)

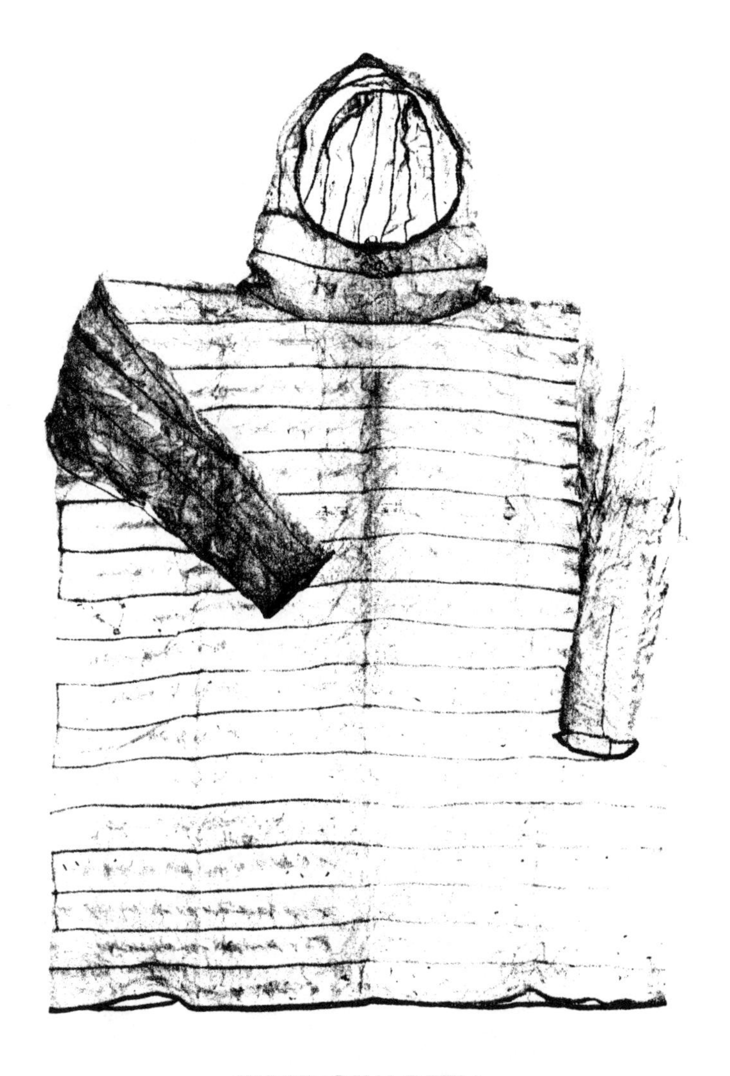

HUNTING KAMLEIKA
Etholen Collection, Helsinki

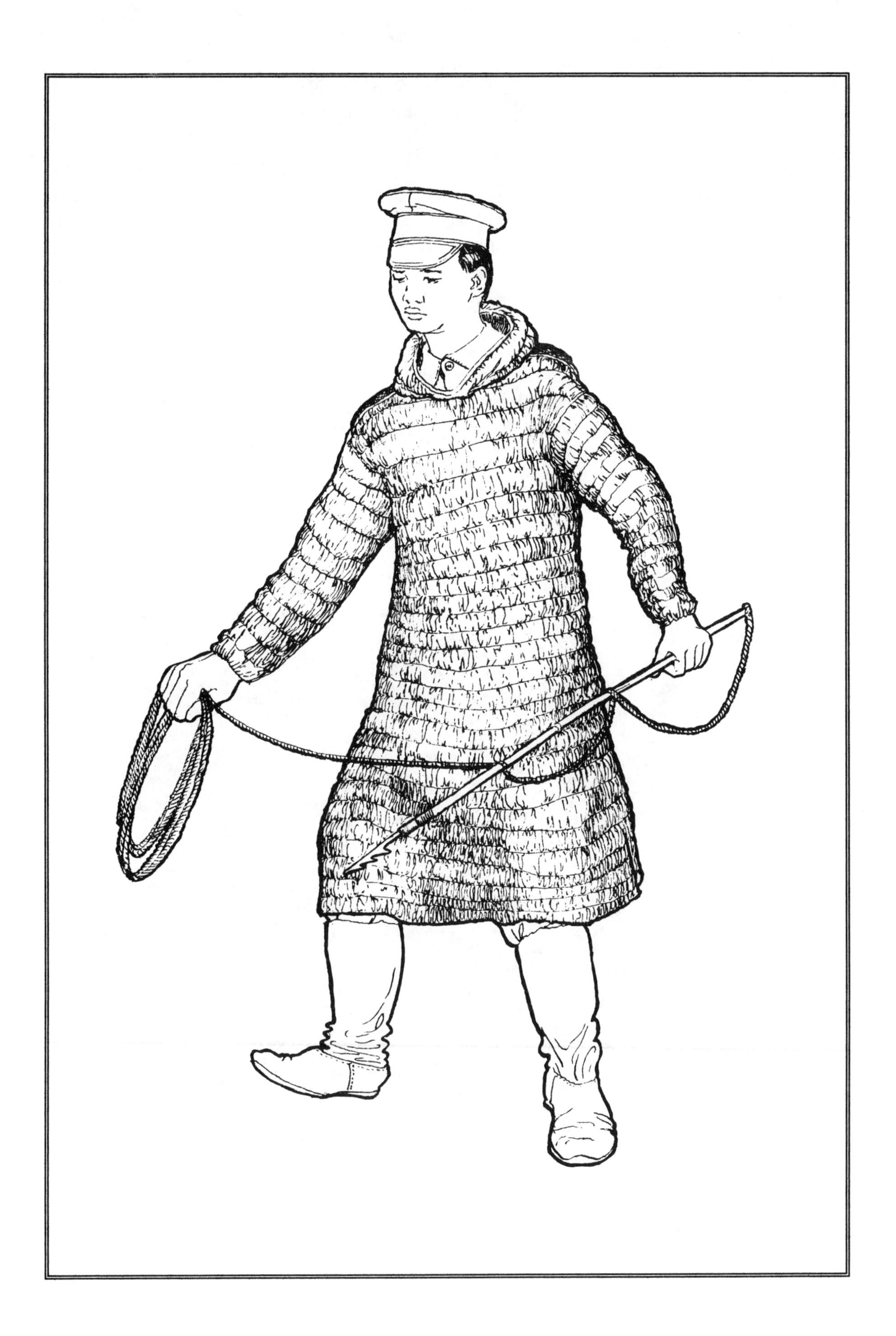

RECONSTRUCTION
(Illustration by John Middleton)

An employee's wife next to the stove. The small cap, made often of colored silk or fine linen, was worn under the scarf which entirely covered the head when outdoors. The dress is a simple cloth print dress typical of working women's dresses of the 1830s. Evidently corsets with stays were not common in the colonies, and the dresses hung about the body without the benefit of these devices. Leather ankle boots were worn when outside, and some sort of soft slipper, felt or leather, was worn inside, in the Russian fashion.

Concerning calico, etc. Calico, semi-calico and printed linens are generally used in the colonies. Even the Aleuts have grown fond of using this cloth, and therefore it has become one of the necessary demands for women's clothes. Calico is used by the families of officials and clerks; the semi-calico is used by the promyshlenniks and Aleuts. (Khlebnikov, 94; 202)

RESIST PRINT FABRIC

RECONSTRUCTION
(Illustration by John Middleton)

A Company employee in "festive dress". The jacket, trousers, and waist coat were made from "soldier's cloth", a black green frieze. The cap was made from the same material. A black silk cravat is tied around the linen European shirt, and leather straps attached to the hem of the trousers are worn under the instep of the black leather boots. The buttons could be either plain brass military surplus type, or a silvered civil type with a discreet pattern stamped on the front.

Concerning broadcloth. During Mr. Baranov's management of the colonies, frieze was generally used to make clothing; soon after it was replaced by linen; good soldier's linen and the ordinary type of linen are comfortable for worker's clothing. Russian and Aleut promyshlenniks buy them willingly; but there is a competition among them because they want to have the best clothing for the holidays; that is why it is necessary to have linens of average prices; let us say 6 to 10 rubles per sazhen. Colors most used are blue and grey. The grey, dark-green, black and blue linens must also be of a high quality; part of them are needed in California. (Khlebnikov; 94; 204)

COMPANY SAILOR (CADET), 1851, *POLNOE SOBRANIE ZAKONOV*

FEMALE LABORERS' CLOTHING FROM RUSSIAN SOURCES, 1830s - 1840s

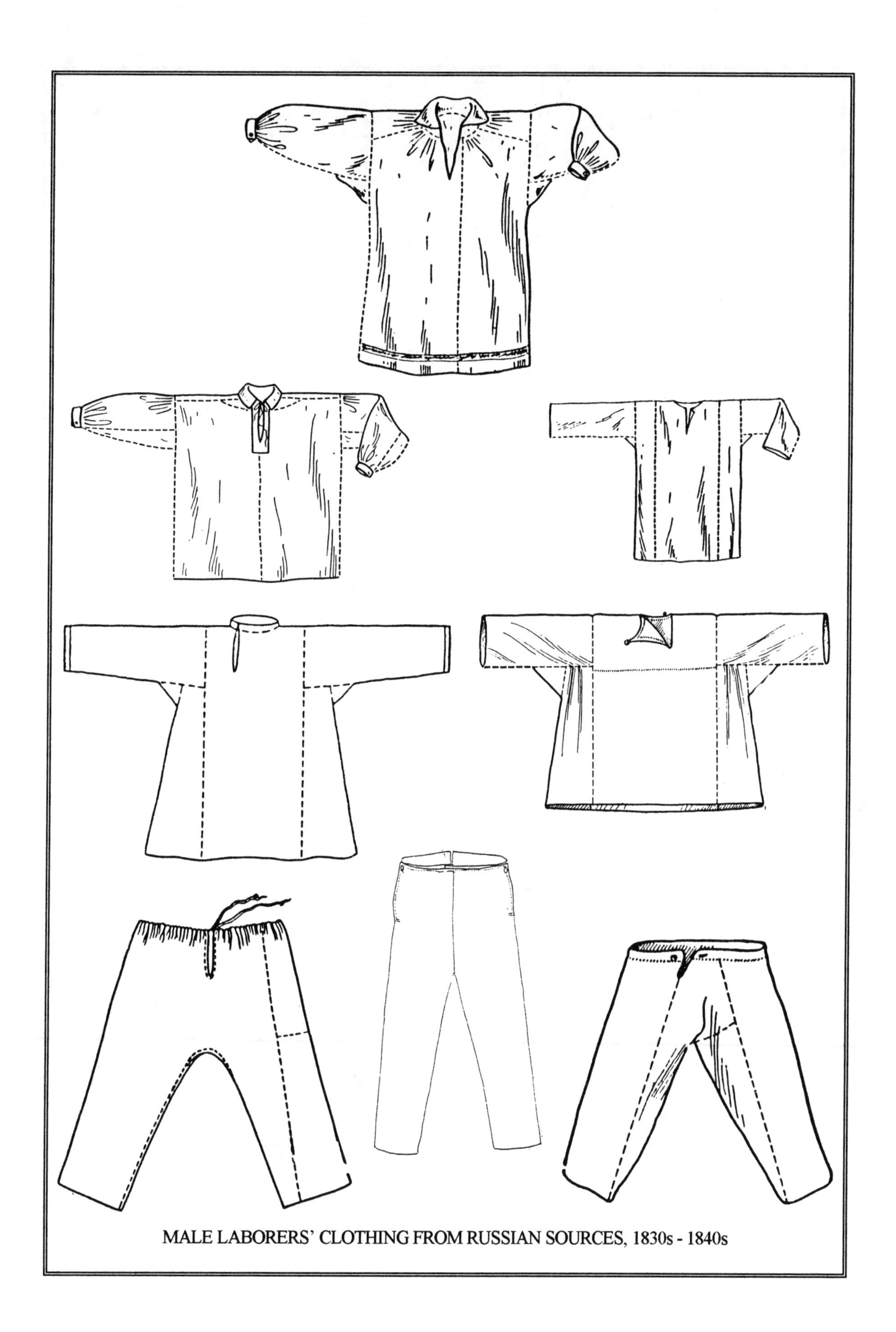

MALE LABORERS' CLOTHING FROM RUSSIAN SOURCES, 1830s - 1840s

MALE LABORERS' CLOTHING FROM RUSSIAN SOURCES, 1830s - 1840s

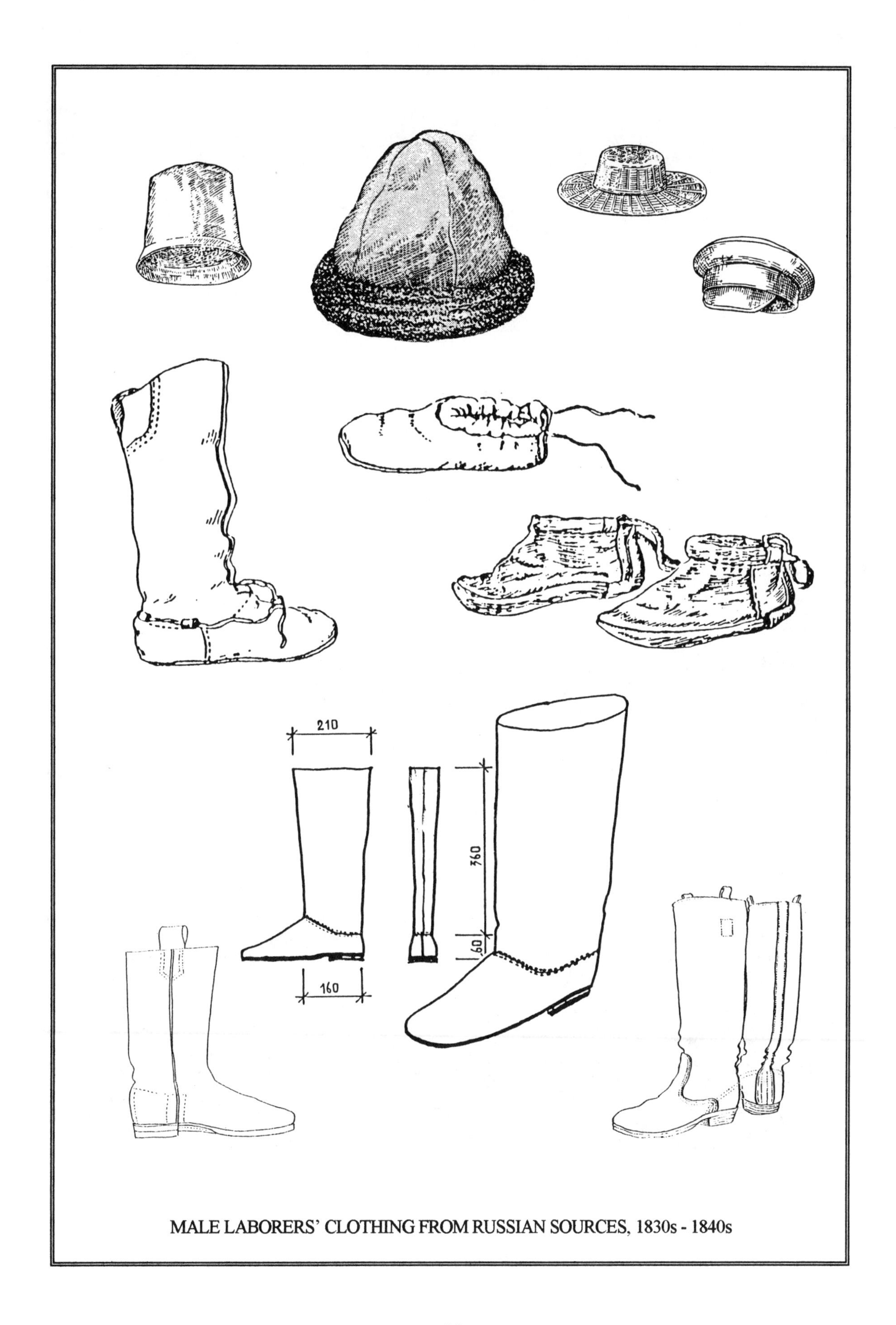

MALE LABORERS' CLOTHING FROM RUSSIAN SOURCES, 1830s - 1840s

SITKA HARBOR (detail)
Artist Unknown

ILLUSTRATIONS OF NAVY AND MERCHANT SHIPPERS

KRONSHTADT ROAD (detail of boat crew in red shirts), I. K. Aivazovsky, 1840

Il'ia Voznesenskii on board the company ship *Naslednik Aleksandr* in the Gulf of California in 1842 described the four creole rowers of the Captain's gig as wearing red shirts, *"A gig was lowered, and the captain, the supercargo and I set out for shore under an awning, as they do in the tropics. With four rowers in red shirts (from the creoles) deftly pulling the oars, we flew rapidly towards the shore and through the rocks rolled in with the surf to a sandy beach."* (Alekseev; 87; 28) These were exactly like the boat crew's uniforms worn at the same time by the Imperial navy.

RECONSTRUCTION

(Illustration by Viktor N. Malyshev)

The **sailor on the left**, in "working rig" wears the black wool, piped in white, sailor's forage cap. The numbers in either yellow thread or painted on the band designate the company of the Ekipazh. The shirt and trousers were made of linen sailcloth or blue cotton "doba", either a twill or plain weave. The blue shirt was sometimes worn with the white trousers. Trousers were worn inside the boots for work detail. A piece of rope or leather belt was worn on the outside of the shirt.

The central figure wears the leather shako worn by fleet sailors in the 1830s. The crossed anchors were in stamped brass, as were the numerals below which showed the ekipazh number. The black jacket could have black or white shoulder straps and sleeve flaps, white piping along collar and cuffs, or be entirely black, depending upon ekipazh. The boatswain's pipe and silver chain worn around the neck, and the gold wide braid around the collar and cuffs indicate a **petty officer**. The trousers were white linen in summer, and black wool in winter. Trousers were always worn over the boots with this form of dress.

The sailor on the right wears the light grey brown greatcoat of the navy. The greatcoat was worn as a coat often, rather than as an overcoat, with only shirt and trousers underneath. Medals were always worn on the greatcoat. The naval coat had a black collar, sometimes plain, sometimes with collar tabs, or with white piping. Brass buttons with plain anchors were worn by the fleet, double headed eagles upon crossed anchors were worn by the Guard's Ekipazh. The boots were made with the suede side out, and were blackened and brushed to give them a dull polish.

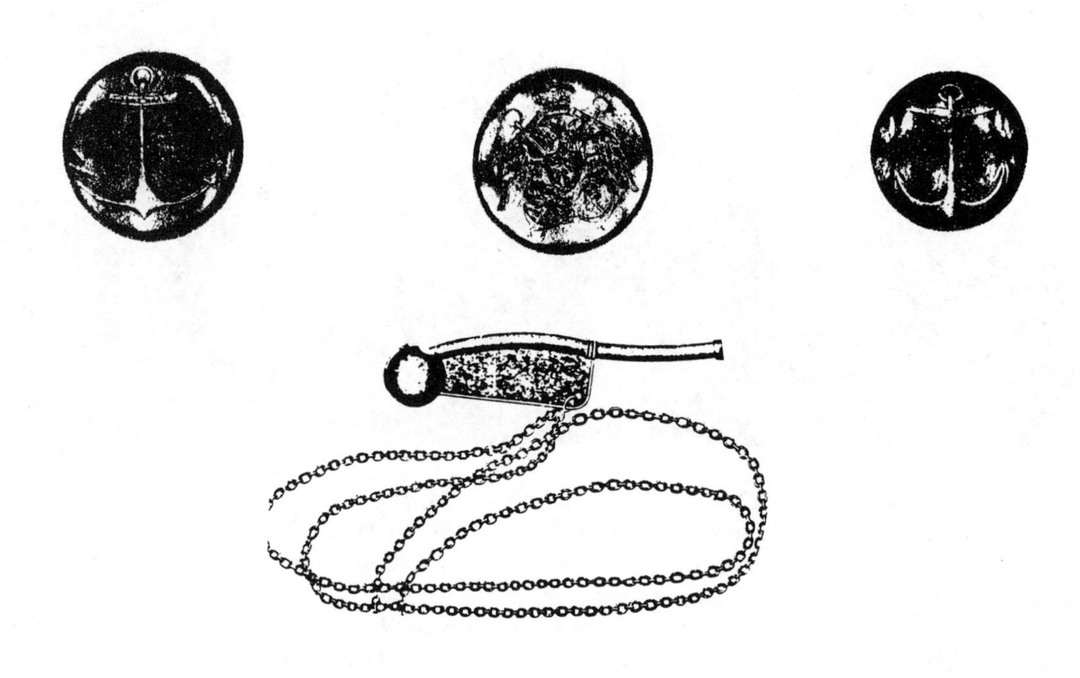

RECONSTRUCTION

Edited drawings taken from the 1851 published regulations for the ship's uniforms of the Russian-American Company. The anchors on the collars and the officer's kortik and belt have been removed. Although technically ten years too late for the Fort Ross period (1812-1841), the style of the clothing illustrated is none the less typical of the late 1830s. The long collars, rear flap pockets with buttons beneath, and the narrow sleeve with flaring cuff are consistent with the 1830s in Russia. The 1851 regulation calls for the coats and jackets and trousers to be made with black green wool broadcloth, piped in blue or violet, the same combination for later merchant marine services in Russia. These original resource drawings are presented here as reconstructions because of the editing mentioned above. The originals can be found in the 1851 edition of the *Polnoe sobranie zakonov.*

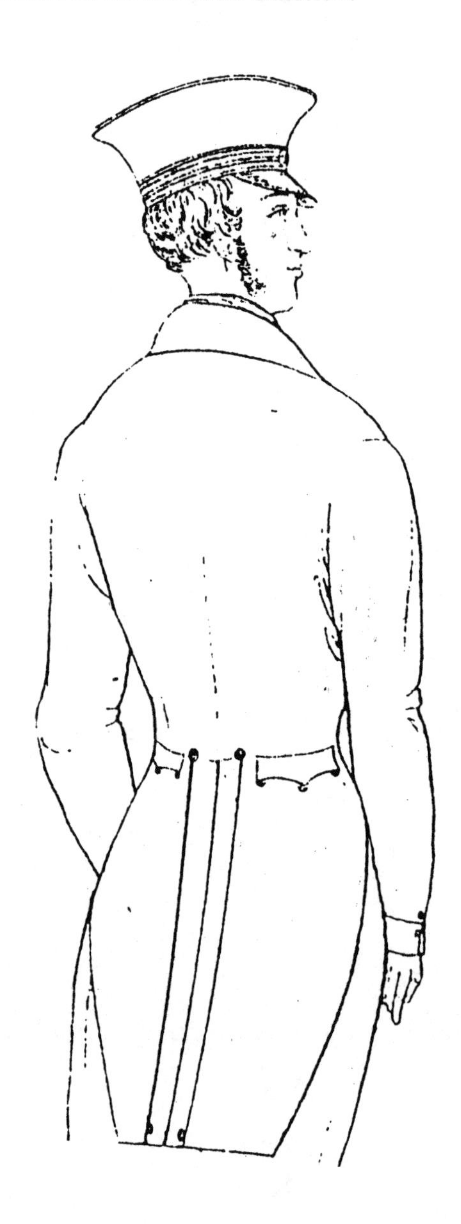

RECONSTRUCTION

(Illustration by Viktor N. Malyshev)

This reconstruction is taken from the Pavel Mikhailov drawing of sailors in a boat crew in the South Pacific in 1827. The figure here wears the black and white forage cap and white cotton or linen shirt. When worn with the jacket the collar is usually left standing, and the black silk tie is worn as a cravat or stock. Here the shirt, worn usually tucked into the trousers, is worn outside. The trousers are the white broadfalls worn over the boots. A casual look for hot weather.

OARSMEN FROM THE CUTTER OF THE 3RD NAVAL DIVISION, 1843
RUSSIAN NAVAL UNIFORMS 1696-1917

РУБАХА РАБОЧАЯ

СЪ БРЮКАМИ ИЗЪ РАВЕНДУКА ИЛИ ПАРУСИНЫ № 7.

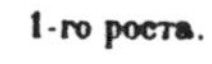

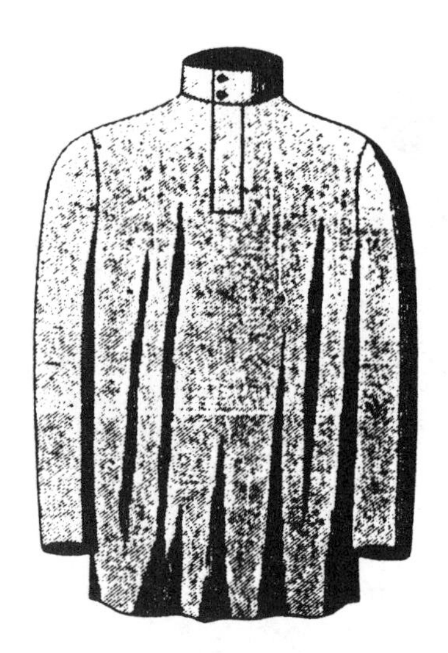

ПОДШТАННИКИ. НАТѢЛЬНАЯ РУБАШКА.

2-го роста.

NAVAL CLOTHING, 1830s - 1840s

WORK UNIFORM reproduced from an undated 19th century naval uniform manual. These show the linen sailcloth work outfit of the sailor in the 1830's. UNDERWEAR is underdrawers and the distinctive blue and white knit sailors undershirt.

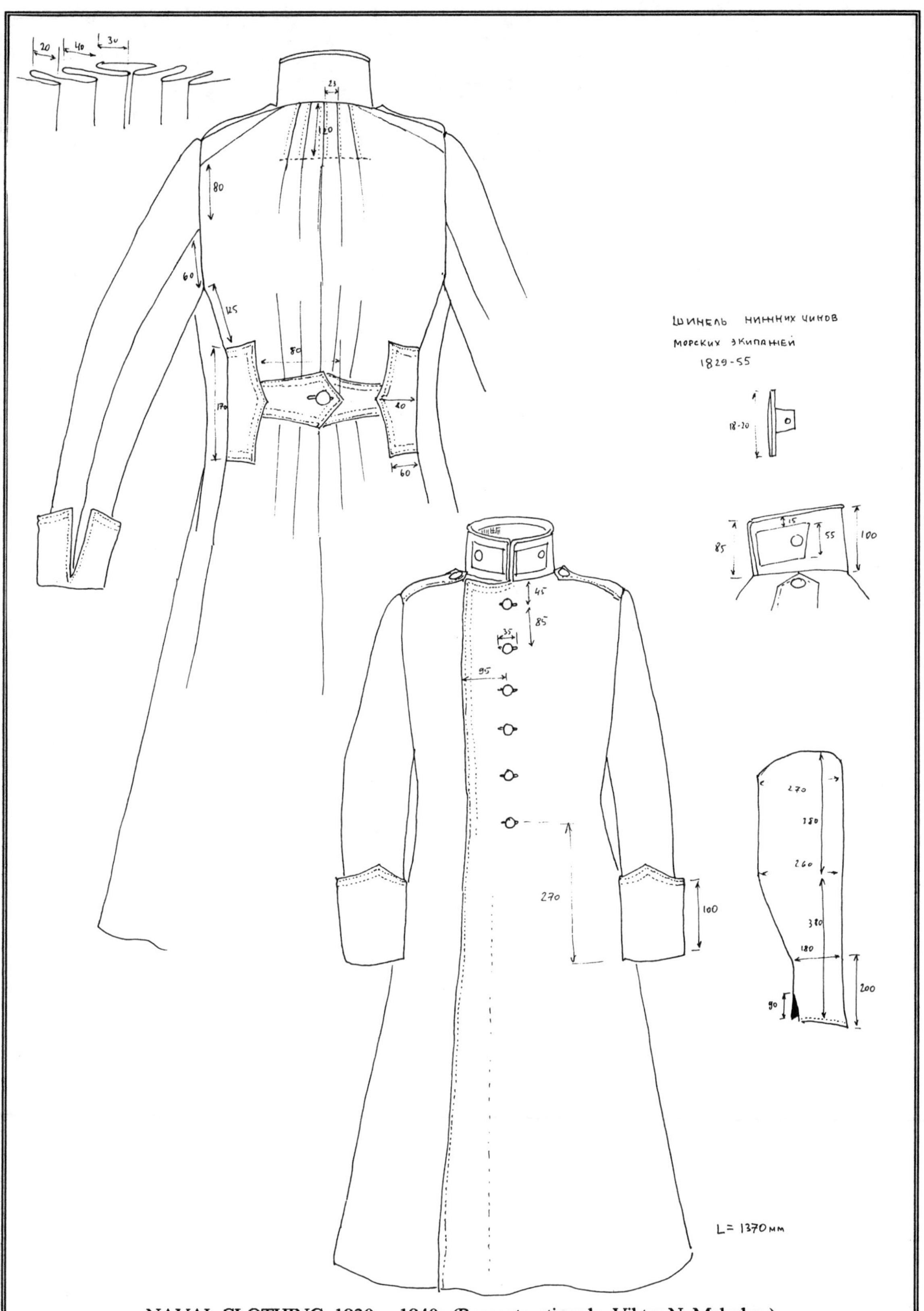

NAVAL CLOTHING, 1830s - 1840s (Reconstructions by Viktor N. Malyshev)
SAILOR'S GREATCOAT, grey brown (mud) colored rough wool coat, black collar with white piping, white collar tabs and black shoulder straps.

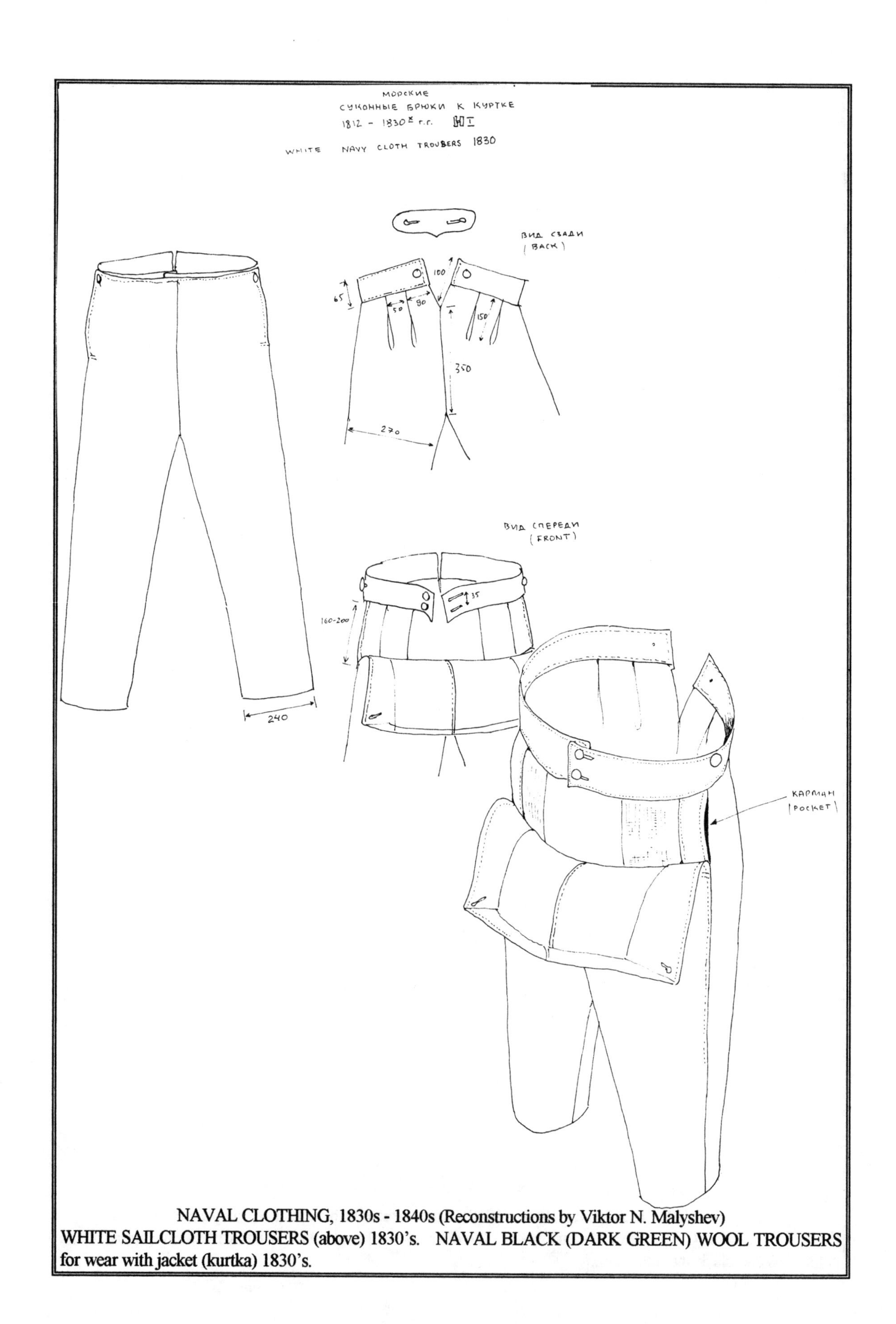

NAVAL CLOTHING, 1830s - 1840s (Reconstructions by Viktor N. Malyshev)
WHITE SAILCLOTH TROUSERS (above) 1830's. NAVAL BLACK (DARK GREEN) WOOL TROUSERS for wear with jacket (kurtka) 1830's.

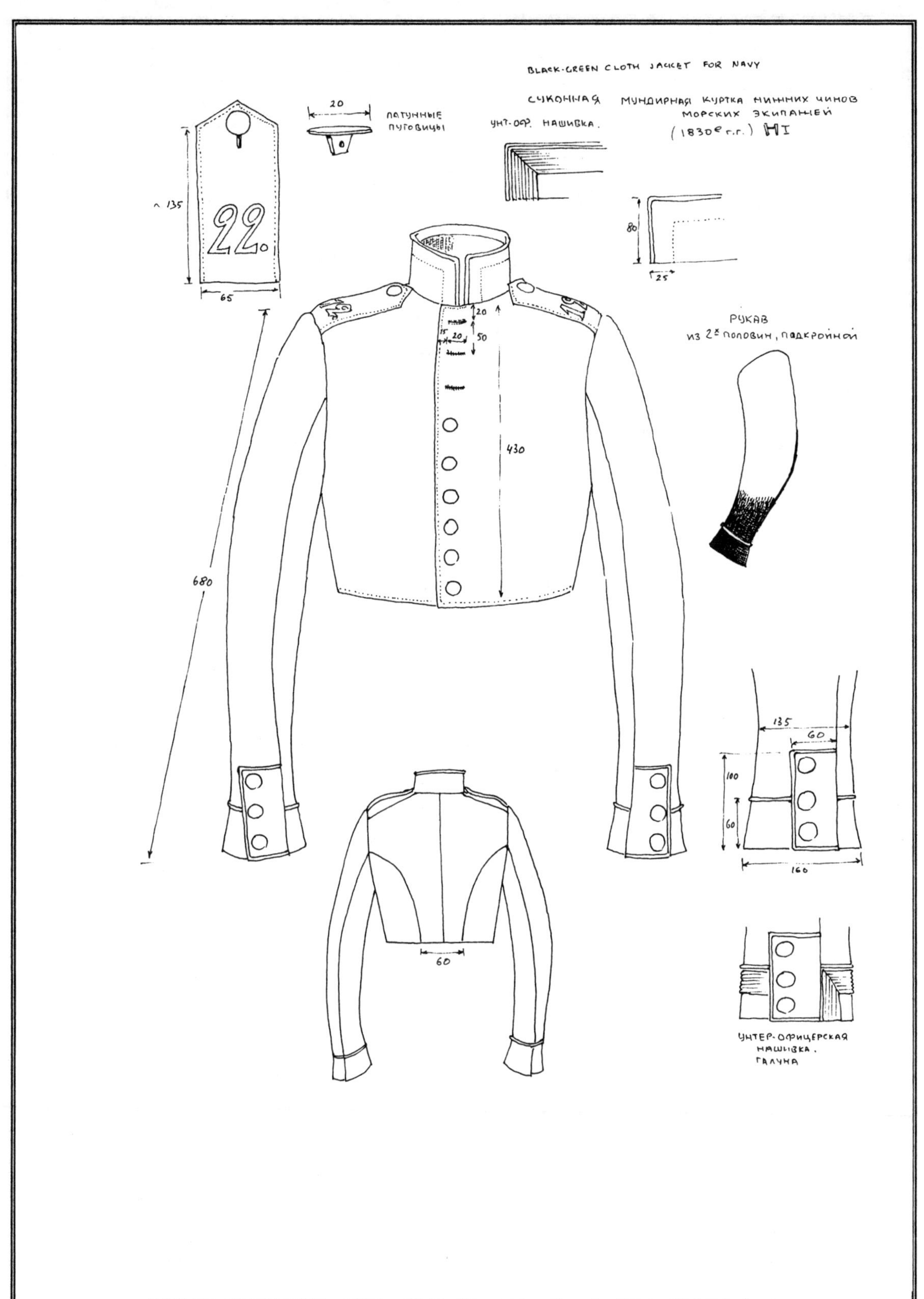

NAVAL CLOTHING, 1830s - 1840s (Reconstructions by Viktor N. Malyshev)
KURTKA (SAILOR'S BLACK WOOL JACKET) with white piping around collar and cuffs, plain brass buttons, yellow cloth or painted numerals on black (red for guard crews) shoulder straps.

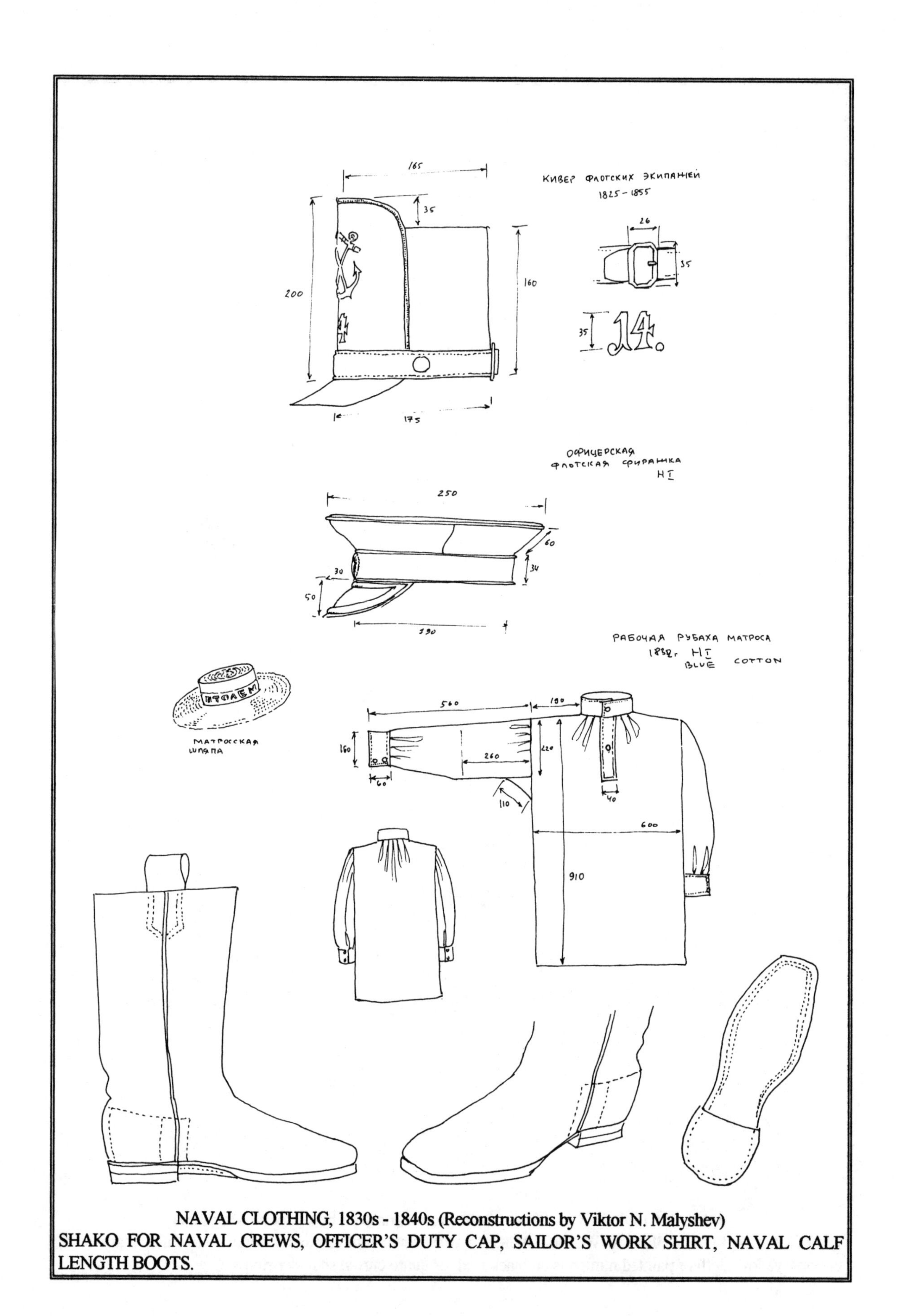

NAVAL CLOTHING, 1830s - 1840s (Reconstructions by Viktor N. Malyshev)
SHAKO FOR NAVAL CREWS, OFFICER'S DUTY CAP, SAILOR'S WORK SHIRT, NAVAL CALF LENGTH BOOTS.

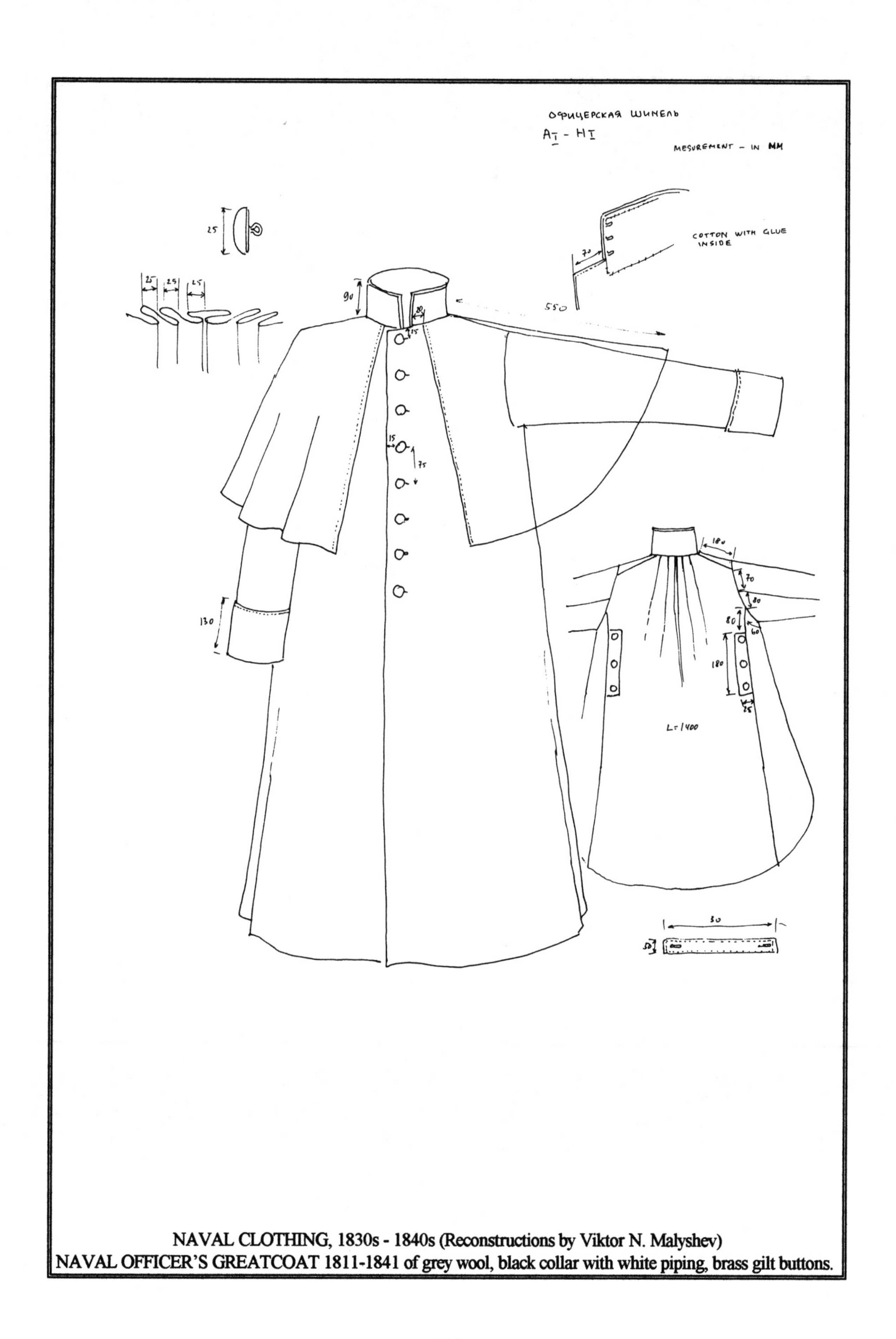

NAVAL CLOTHING, 1830s - 1840s (Reconstructions by Viktor N. Malyshev)
NAVAL OFFICER'S GREATCOAT 1811-1841 of grey wool, black collar with white piping, brass gilt buttons.

FORT ROSS CLOTHING: NEW DATA FROM OLD SOURCES

By Lynne Goldstein
Department of Anthropology, University of Wisconsin-Milwauke
Photographs by Alan Magayne-Roshak

Introduction

The Fort Ross Cemetery project (excavations 1990-1992) has yielded a wealth of information about Fort Ross and the people who lived and died there. While we anticipated some of the kinds of information we found, other types were a surprise. In particular, we have been pleased by the amount of information we have gathered on clothing and clothing manufacturing techniques.

Any discussion of this material must begin with a word of caution, however: The analysis of the Fort Ross Cemetery data is now underway, and much of the material has not yet been properly cleaned - what is included here is therefore preliminary and subject to some changes. Nonetheless, we can make some general statements about a mundane item like button attachments.

What We've Found

The easiest way to summarize our findings is to list clothing-related items by category. For each category, I've provided a brief summary of the kinds of things we've recovered, as well as a comment or two on what's unusual, important, or surprising.

Crosses and medallions. Most individuals were buried with a cross or a medallion with a cross on it. Although this is nearly a constant across the site, there is a considerable amount of variability in the size and style of crosses and medallions - silver, copper, and various metal alloys were used. Some crosses were quite fancy, and others very plain. It is likely that the crosses and medallions we found were ones that were worn by the individual throughout his or her life.

Beads. The quantity and variability in the types of glass trade beads represented at the cemetery (primarily from Czechoslovakia, Venice, and China) are impressive and significant. It is unusual to find beads in their primary context, so that you can determine how they were used. For example, in three instances, we have almost identically fashioned earrings or ear ornaments. Beads of similar color and size are used in a distinctive pattern in each case to create the earring. In other instances, we have evidence of single and multi-strand necklaces, as well as beads sewn on clothing, beaded bags, and medallions or pouches. Beads are placed on clothing at the neckline, in interesting patterns, and also occasionally in a line along the pants leg or skirt. We found two elaborately beaded pouches or bags with infant burials, and we have also found evidence of a round, beaded "medallion" or pouch worn at the waist. More details on the assortment and patterns of beads will have to await further analysis.

Buttons. Some of the buttons we've recovered are obviously part of a uniform, while others are non-military in nature. We anticipate that we will eventually be able to identify the jackets more precisely as to military rank and/or other status. The metal buttons are usually found in place, representing double-breasted jackets. The buttons have a wide range in size. An interesting item in several graves is the combination of buttons with trade beads. As has been documented in other instances, these might represent Alaska natives who received old uniforms from the Russians, then decorated and transformed them with beads and other objects.

In at least one instance, we have evidence for what we think are buttons manufactured by recycling old metal. One small metal button has an elaborate design on it. This design would not have been visible unless someone got quite close to the individual. Further, the design is unfinished and cut off at the edge of the button. Our best guess is that the metal was originally part of something else, and was later made into buttons.

Most of the buttons we've found are metal with a shank or loop attachment - sometimes the button is decorated, sometimes not. In a few graves, we've also found white glass buttons. Although most of these buttons are four-hole, a few have only three holes. It is not clear if these glass buttons were attached to shirts or dresses or something else.

Burial clothing and textiles. Most individuals were apparently wrapped in shrouds; metal in the grave, whether in the form of crosses or other items, often preserves a section of this fabric. The shrouds, however, often cover items of clothing. Most of the fabric is linen, however, in several instances we have portions of wool jackets and coats, as well as linings. I will focus on the fabric from two graves in the next section of this paper.

Other items. We recovered a creamware bowl and some English blue and white porcelain cups and saucers from a grave. These were placed at the head, along with a number of other items. From other graves, we have recovered several metal hair ornaments, fragments of chains (a watch fob and chain?), small bottles, a mirror, a spoon, thimbles, etc.

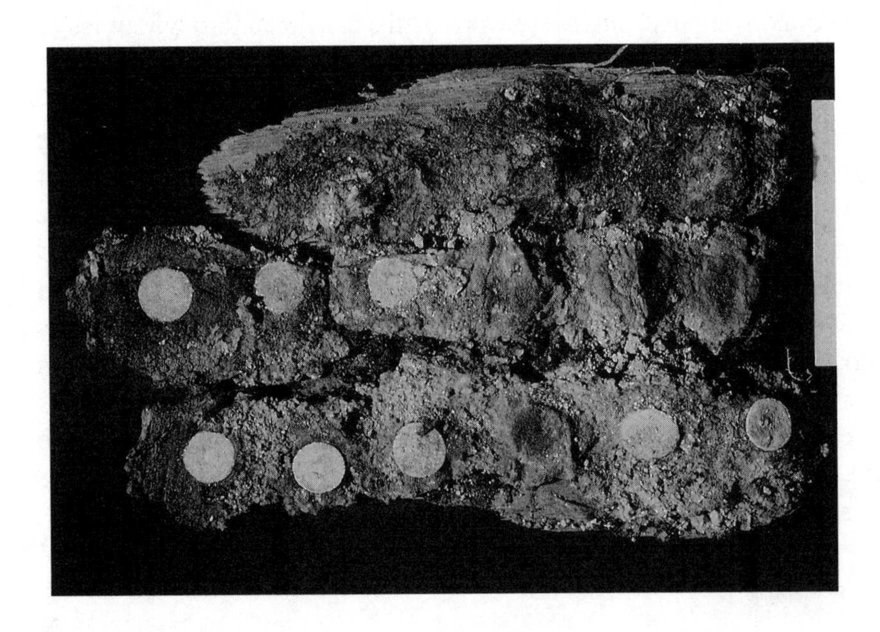

Figure 1
Feature 116

.A Look at How Buttons are Attached

Two graves at the cemetery provide us with a level of detail about clothing manufacture that has been unanticipated. The two graves are labeled Feature 116 and Feature 73.

Feature 116 was the grave of an adult male, and included an impressive double-breasted coat with large buttons and a silver watch chain. At this initial stage of analysis, it does not appear that the coat is a military coat, but more likely something that a businessman might wear. The buttons are metal and have elaborate designs, and the coat is a heavy dark green wool, with a lighter brownish green silk (?) lining. As you can see from the first photograph (Figure 1), much of the coat was preserved.

The next three photographs show close-up views of the buttons on the coat. Figure 2 shows some of the detail design on the button, as well as the fact that the button was still attached to the fabric. In Figure 3, the button is turned over and several important features are visible: 1) a hole was punched through the fabric and the shank or loop of the button was pushed through this hole; 2) a leather thong was threaded through the button shank or loop once the button was in place; and 3) the leather thong itself was sewn onto the fabric. This would seem to make for a sturdier button attachment than the approach we use today. Figure 4 shows another button from the coat, along with a small ecru disk that serves some unknown purpose. As yet, we have no idea whether it is associated with coat manufacture, represents some kind of bead, or is something else entirely. the photograph provided another close-up of both the button detail and the fabric weave.

Figure 2 (top), 3 (middle) and 4 (bottom)
All Feature 116

Feature 73 yielded more cloth than any other grave in the cemetery. The fabric provides more information on button attachments, and has also yielded our first glimpse of some fine plaid fabric. Figure 5 shows an assortment of fabrics of different weaves and textures, and at the righthand edge of the fabric, you can see another thong button attachment. Figures 6 and 7 are reverse sides of another piece of fabric, and shows several things in detail: 1) a common fabric weave; 2) a good finished edge; and 3) another button attachment.

Figures 8 and 9 are also reverse sides of an edge piece of fabric with buttons attached. This time, however, several buttons are in place and the reverse side (Figure 9) makes it clear that a long leather thong could be used to attach a line of buttons in such cases. Note that the outside fabric is coarser that the inside; note also that the edge of this piece is very well finished, with the two different types of fabric sewn to each other.

The final photograph (Figure 10) shows an exceptionally finely woven cotton or linen fabric that is white with a fine blue plaid. The fabric itself is also woven into a distinctive "white-on-white" plaid pattern. To our knowledge, this is the first example of such fine patterned fabric specifically documented for Fort Ross. Whether it was part of an item of clothing, a handkerchief, or something else, we don't really know.

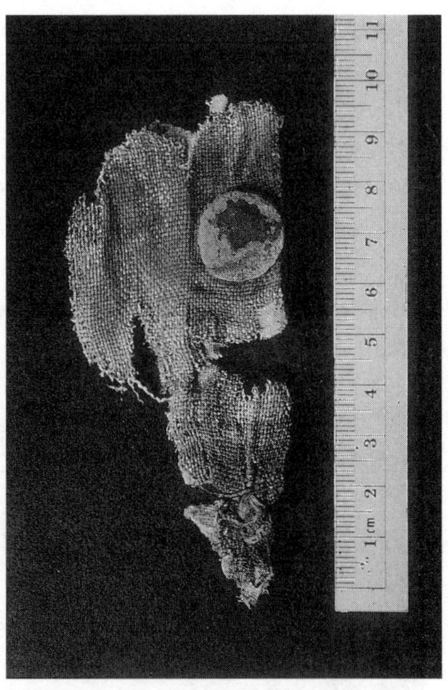

The above discussion provides a tantalizing, but preliminary glimpse into what we have learned about clothing from the Fort Ross Cemetery. We have a long way to go in our analysis, but what we have learned thus far suggests that the work will be productive in adding to the rich details of life at Fort Ross.

Figures 5 (top), 6 (middle) and 7 (bottom)
All Feature 73

Figure 8 (top), 9 (middle)
and 10 (bottom)
All Feature 73

RUSSIAN AMERICAN COMPANY LISTS DETAILING FABRIC AND CLOTHING AVAILABLE IN THE COLONIES

From *RUSSIAN AGENCIES. BARON FERDINAND VON WRANGELL'S REPORT, APRIL 10, 1834:*

EXPENSE ACCOUNT OF A RUSSIAN PROMYSHLENNIK AT FORT ROSS: VASILY PERMITIN (1832)

...To give some idea of a Russian promyshlennik's expenditures at Fort Ross, I include here the accounts of one of them, Vasily Permitin, who has a wife and five children. During the year 1832 he received on account:

...felt	2 rolls
cotton stockings	1 pair
woolen blankets	2 rolls
cotton cloth	1 roll
soles	21 pairs
boot vamps	10 pairs
Nankeen cloth	5 pieces
medium-sized sheepskins	2 pieces
Flemish linen	48 feet
calico	73.5 feet
ticking	39 feet
misc. [cloth]	34.5 feet
gingham	16 feet
soldier's broadcloth	5.5 feet

From *COLONIAL RUSSIAN AMERICA, KYRILL T. KHLEBNIKOV'S REPORTS, 1817-1832.*

[Brought on the *Juno*, paid for by the Californians, 1806, p. 114]
Flemish cloth
sail cloth
heavy wool
cotton goods
needles
boots of Siberian leather
ticking

[Goods received by Baranov from Canton, 1810, for sale in the colonies, p. 13]
4,000 pieces of nankeen
2,000 blue Chinese cotton
800 unbleached Chinese cotton
200 bombazine
600 cotton
10 velvet
250 demicotton
10 pikols thread. . .
55 bolts seersucker
595 silk gilets
500 bolts silk
500 bolts silk
200 bolts silk
147 bolts atlas satin
50 cases kerchiefs
170 bolts satin
50 bolts satin
30 bolts taffeta
28 katti silk
5 bolts raw wool camelot. . .
unbleached Chinese cotton, bolt
unglazed red Chinese cotton
black Chinese cotton
demicotton
white bombazine
first quality Bengal
third quality Bengal
fourth quality Bengal
velvet
thread, pound
seersucker. . .
taffeta
fine Chinese silk
atlas satin
flowered satin

black satin
blue satin
fabric for an ensenble
Chinese kancha silk
serge suit
silk

[Goods in Russian America received from foreign exchange received 1818, p. 19]
1,550 bolts blue Chinese cotton
48 bolts black Chinese cotton
165 bolts cotton
360 black serge kerchiefs
1,664 Bengal cotton kerchiefs
1,180 second quality Bengal kerchiefs
1,467 arshins frieze
712 arshins low quality cloth
822 arshins frieze
556 arshins flannel
1,596 arshins bombazine
400 frieze blankets
45 bolts Canton silk. . .
115 English leather soles. . .
290 bolts Bengal and Canton calico

[Required clothing for 30 pupils in New Arkhangel, 1820, p.47]
1 set warm grey woolen clothing lined with crash, 30 sets
1 set summer clothing made of ticking, 30
3 fur hats apiece, 90
3 linen shirts apiece, 90
1 cap apiece, 30
3 arshins crash, for leggings, 90 sets

[Items on 1825 company price list for sale to inhabitants of the colonies, p.71]
thread
rawhide
soles for shoes. . .
Chinese Kiakhta cloth, large
Chinese Canton cloth, large
large American blanket
small American blanket
large English blanket
medium English blanket
frieze, good quality
frieze, medium quality
frieze, kalmuk
English calico, good quality
English calico, medium quality
Russian calico
good English wool
Dutch wool
ordinary wool
wool for sailors' uniforms
wool for soldiers' uniforms
wool calico
bengal, for lining pockets
men's cotton stockings
women's cotton stockings
knit stockings
woolen stockings
leggings
striped ticking
heavy blue ticking
Flemish cloth
sailcloth

As of January 1826 there was a large quantity of Russian and foreign goods in the warehouses [in the colonies] which had been brought in during 1825 from St. Petersburg and from England aboard the ship *Elena*, and a full ship's cargo was purchased from the American Blanchard. . [p.84]

English woolens
154 arshins
316 arshins
1,533 arshins
2,018 arshins
1,260 arshins
2,095 arshins woolen cloth
5,900 arshins kalmuk cloth
3,183 arshins various friezes
3,965 archins large blankets
1,532 arshins small blankets

1,329 bolts Chinese cotton
3,358 arshins various calicos
284 bolts calico, *kolenkor*
1,907 arshins calico, mitkal
2,837 bolts various fabrics
1,286 pairs stockings
23 1/2 puds thread
55,808 arshins various linens
42,160 arshins ticking and sheeting
240 puds yarn. . .

From *KHLEBNIKOV ACHIVE, TRAVEL NOTES 1820, 1822 AND 1824)*

[Goods purchased from Mr. Newell on the *Mentor* for Fort Ross, 1824, p 148]
. . . 10 pieces of cotton cloth
12 pieces of cotton cloth
25 pieces of crepe
20 pieces, 160 cotton kerchiefs
2 pieces, 40 serge kerchiefs
10 pieces, 70 plain serge kerchiefs
5 pieces, 100 plain serge kerchiefs
10 dozen bundles of silk thread
20 bundles of thread
20 pieces of white mitkal calico
20 pieces of blue mitkal calico. . .
50 pieces of mitkal calico
25 silk hats. . .
7 1/2 yards of red cloth
20 1/2 yards of blue cloth
27 1/2 yards of dark cloth
21 yards of cashmere
44 1/2 yards of cashmere
20 bundles, 400 serge kerchiefs. . .

[Goods delivered on the *Buldakov*, 1820, for sale in California, p.72]
Silk, Cotton, and Linen Articles
cherry colored nankeen
white nankeen
first quality cotton cloth
second quality cotton cloth
wide Flemish cloth
ordinary gray Flemish cloth
taffeta
foulard
satin
first quality canvas, wide
second quality canvas, thin
black serge cloths
first quality muslin kerchiefs
second quality muslin kerchiefs
cotton kerchiefs. . .
gingham
cotton thread
patent thread
fine thread
thread for cuffs
muslin
sittsy calico
first quality ribbon
scond quality ribbon
third quality ribbon
double worsted braid
ordinary worsted braid
half cotton worsted braid
cotton worsted braid
silk stockings
Haberdashery
silk fans
first quality watch chain
second quality watch chain
stamp, carried on watch chain
keys, carried on watch chain
buttons for uniform
small buttons
package of pins
first quality earrings
second quality earrings

[Taken for trade in California on the *Buldakov*, 1820, p.62]
50 pieces of simple cotton fabric with cherry colored edging
200 small pieces of nankeen
10 wide pieces of Bengalese linen
4 pieces of Cantonese linen

7 pieces of bombazine
5 pieces of taffeta
6 pieces of foulard
2 fabric tablecloths
20 yards of gingham
80 Cantonese kerchiefs
2 dozen white napkins
20 black serge kerchiefs
61 arshins of thick red cloth
85 yards of red flannelette
2 English hats
166 1/2 arshins of thin linen
255 1/2 arshins of thick linen
108 1/2 arshins of linen for napkins
50,000 needles. . .

From *CORRESPONDENCE OF THE GOVERNORS, COMMUNICATIONS SENT; 1818*

No. 48 Proposal to the NA office, [gifts to toion proposed by Baranov, p. 25]
For toion Genarei:
shoes [*bashmaki*], 2 pair
half boots[*sapogi*], short, 1 pair
cloth [*sukno*] medium, for dress, 4 arshins
For his wife:
boots [*torbasy*], 2
nankeen[*kitaika*] for a shirt [*kamleia*]
green baize [*baika*] for [?]
motley [*pestredi*], 20 arshins
metal buttons, 2 1/2 sets [*portishcha*]
silk for sewing, 6 skeins [*motok*]. . .
motley [*pestredi*], 21 arshins. . .
For the [toion's] attendant [*prisluzhnik]:*
shoes, 1 pair
motley,14 arshins
stockings, 1 pair
cloth, ordinary, for jacket [*na ku*. . incomplete word; it was probably *na kurtku*, for a jacket] and trousers, or ready made ones

For Vasilii Moller:
nankeen, 2 ends
silk, 2 skeins. . .

Please send me various Canton goods. . .
kanf [*kanifas* - dimity?], black, white, and light blue [*goluboi*]
Kitaika [*nankeen*], blue- wide, black, light blue- wide,white [*blanzhevykh*]- wide and narrow. . .
silk, spun [*suchenyi*], of various colors, mainly dark. . .
kerchiefs, cloth, of better quality
kerchiefs, cloth, of second quality
buttons, mother-of-pearl, smallest. . .
Chinese silk [*kancha*] of various colors

No. 203 To the commandant of the fort [Ross]. . . The list of things given by the NA office for equipping the three Sandwich Islanders [who were sent to Ross, p. 119]:
3 shirts, 3 pantaloons both Gaizlovskoi pestriadi [striped linen ticking]
45 arshins of ticking for shirts
3 cotton kerchiefs of Petersburg cloth
9 pair of soldiers shoes [bashmakov soldatskikh, ditto - of St. Petersburg]
14 arshins of Flemish linen, of which were made one jacket and one pair of trousers for each
15 arshins of canvas [kanifas], to which, because of shortage, were added 3 arshins from the quantity assigned for use aboard ships, altogether 18 arshins, out of which were made a Holland shirt with trousers for each.

BENGAL

(Bengal stripe)

A wide variety of cloths imported from the Bengal region of India, usually silk or a cotton and silk blend. The fabric, which resembled muslin, was usually striped with either printed or woven stripes. Reproduced in England in the early nineteenth century, these striped ginghams were found in a variety of printed fabrics.

BOMBAZINE

(bombazeen)

A twill cloth made of a silk warp and worsted weft, primarily produced in Norwich, England. Often mentioned as a suitable cloth for mourning, bombazines were dyed black after being taken from the loom.

CALICO

A cotton cloth of plain weave produced in a wide variety of printed designs. Originally produced in Calicut, India, calicos were first printed in London about 1676. In 1804 they were described by Thomas Sheraton, "*Calicos are of different kinds, plain, printed, stained, dyed, chintz, muslins, and the like. . .*"(Sheraton; 1804) In Russian America, "*Thin calicos are designated for the officials, while the grey American is used mainly in Sitkha for trade with the Kolosh, who are paid in calico for small for pelts; at Ross, calico is used to pay Indians for working the soil and harvesting grain. The Indians use the calico to wrap themselves in instead of using blankets.* (Khlebnikov; 94; 203)

CALMUC

(kalmuck)

"*Twilled woolen made of loose twist yarn, fulled and finished with a long nap, used as winter dress goods.*" (Harmuth; 1915) Named after a tribe in Central Asia which produced wool from their flocks, this cloth was later produced in a cotton imitation.

CAMLET

(camblet)

Originally a rich fabric of medieval Asia, it was made of camel's hair or angora wool. In the nineteenth century a plain woven cloth made of goat's hair, silk or linen mix, or entirely of wool. Known for its waterproof qualities.

CASHMERE

"*A closely woven, soft, fine and light dress fabric made with single cotton or wool warp and fine Botany filling in a 2-1 weft face twill.*" (Harmuth; 1915) Originally made from the hair of the Kashmir goat, this twill fabric was produced to imitate the light twill tapestry shawls of India.

CASSIMERE

(kerseymere)

Woolen twill, often with a striped pattern, which had a soft texture and medium weight. Also referred to as *kerseymere*, it was developed in England in the late eighteenth century. Used for suiting and furnishings, it was also mixed with silk, cotton or mohair for coats and waistcoats.

CRAPE

A thin, light fabric of silk or cotton which was similar to gauze and often had an irregular weave. It was frequently used in mourning, or as in *crepe de chine* as a material for flags.

CRASH

Coarse cloth. A plain weave fabric, often of linen; used for linings.

DUCK

Linen cloth of a plain weave, lighter than canvas, used for tents, tarpaulins, boat sails, and aprons. It was called duck because of its ability to shed water. Referring to Flemish linen, Khlebnikov wrote, *"In Sitkha it is used to make tents for workers who work in the forests; it is used as a trade item with the Kolosh and to make light summer sailor's clothing; part of it is sold in California. This linen is used by the various offices to mainly make sails for baidaras, tents, clothing for the workers and Aleuts."* (Khlebnikov; 94;204)

FLANNEL

A soft napped fabric made of woolen yarn slightly twisted in the spinning, often with a cotton warp and wool filling. *"Flannelette and flannel is used for winter clothing for the families of officials and workers. . . since there are no pelts, except ground squirrel ones to make winter clothing, the men and women need flannels and flannelettes to make their clothes."* (Khlebnikov; 94; 204)

FOULARD

Printed or checked twill popular for women's dresses or kerchiefs. Produced in England in the nineteenth century, foulard was often misrepresented as being of Indian manufacture.

FRIEZE

Thick woolen cloth with a coarse nap, frequently used for coats and lower class clothing. *"During Mr. Baranov's management of the colonies, frieze was generally used to make clothing; soon after it was replaced by linen. . ."* (Khlebnikov; 94; 204) *". . .friezes and linens have become familiar to the Kolosh since the Northwest Coast became settled by the English and Americans. . ."* (Khlebnikov; 94; 205)

GINGHAM

A cotton cloth woven in plain weave with either checks or stripes. Known for its toughness of texture, it was called *pestriadi* by the Russians and was popularly used for shirts, dresses and skirts.

NANKEEN

Cotton cloth of a plain weave imported from Nankin, China. Nankeen referred to a great variety of cotton cloths available both in Canton and to the Russians in Kiakhta. *"The colonies prefer getting Cantonese nankeen because it is larger in size, and one piece of it is sufficient to make someone a coat or dress, and the price is almost the same as that of calico. When there is no means of getting Cantonese calico, we can get Kiakhta nankeen, which is cherry-colored, glossy and non glossy, and has great breadth. The Russian nankeen brought here on the ship Elena was of good quality, but it faded quickly, and could only be sold when needed. If the color of the cloth becomes more durable and does not fade, it may replace the Cantonese and Kiakhta nankeen. This would be more advantageous because it is cheaper."* (Khlebnikov; 94; 202)

SEERSUCKER

(cirsaka, sirsaka)

Sirsaka, a mixed silk and cotton striped fabric exported from India. It is known for its distinctive texture, having ripples formed in alternating stripes by weaving the cotton warps in looser tension than the silk.

SERGE

Woolen twill with a worsted warp and woolen weft. Available in many varieties and qualities, it was chiefly known as an inexpensive durable cloth for clothing. Denim is a later abbreviation of *serge de nismes.*

TAFFETA

(taffety)

A medium or light weight silk or silk-cotton fabric, often striped or checked with weft threads slightly thicker than warp, and having a crosswise ribbed effect.

TICKING

Linen twill often having a striped design in the weave. *"The promyshlenniks and Koloshes in general use ticking to make their shirts. The type they need are made of inexpensive linen. They rarely use half-cotton or full cotton cloth because of their cost. Ticks and deburets are used to make hospital robes, sheets and light work clothes. The Aleuts especially like these materials. They are also used by the Kenais and Aglegmiuts, who make women's kamleiki out of them; these are exchanged for river otters. In California this material is in general use by the Indians because of its durability and is readily bought at the mission and by the Indians."* (Khlebnikov; 94; 203)

VELVETEEN

Cotton velvet which was patented in England in 1776. In 1833 it was available in every possible color, and was considered superior to the original cotton velvet.

WOOLEN

Broadcloth, or *sukhno* in Russian, was a cloth made of carded short staple fibers, which was shrunk after weaving to produce a denser, heavier fabric. Concerning woolen cloth Khlebnikov wrote, *"The dark green is designated for use by the officials; the red by the Aleuts who use the threads to embellish their kamleika, parkas and baidarkas, etc."* (Khlebnikov; 94; 204)

WORSTED

Woolen thread that is firmly twisted from combed, staple wool fibers of the same length. Worsted cloth has a smooth, hard surface with no nap. Worsted threads are frequently combined with others to produce cloth such as bombazine and serge.

DICTIONARY OF RUSSIAN LANGUAGE WORDS IN TEXT

ARSHIN: Equivalent to 28 inches.

BEZKOZIRKA: Literally "without visor" from furazhka bezkozirka. The standard Russian military forage cap, introduced in 1811, without visor for "other ranks".

DOBA: Blue cotton cloth for work clothing, in either plain weave or drill.

GILET: Man's waistcoat or vest.

KAMLEIKA: Diminutive of kamleia. A gut garment usually in the form of a pull over parka, made in horizontal strips. Worn by baidarka crews as waterproof clothing.

KARTUZ: Wool or linen cloth cap worn by all classes in Russia as a work or casual cap; seldom, except in the lower classes, as a dress cap.

KOSOVOROTKA: Male pull over shirt, with a neck opening off center (most commonly on the wearer's left) and a standing collar, narrow neck band, or no collar at all, with or without cuffs.

KRASHENINA: A coarse woven linen cloth that was often printed with a brightly colored design used for linings.

NARODNYE ODEZHDA: National or folk costume.

PESTRIADI: Fine checked cloth.

SARAFAN: Russian dress of the national style, full length with straps over the shoulder; predominantly worn in north and north central Russia.

SOLDIER'S CLOTH: A black green wool frieze (almost black by 1830's for the navy; dark green for the army).

RED AND WHITE LINEN TICKING FOR SHIRTING
State Russian Ethnographic Museum, St. Petersburg

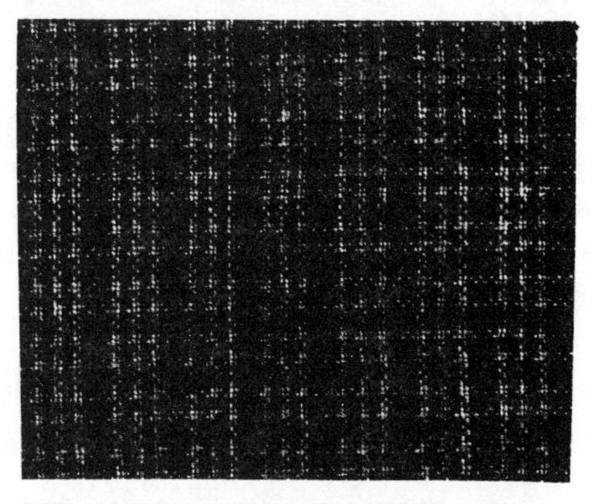

RED AND WHITE LINEN PESTRIADI
State Russian Ethnographic Museum, St. Petersburg

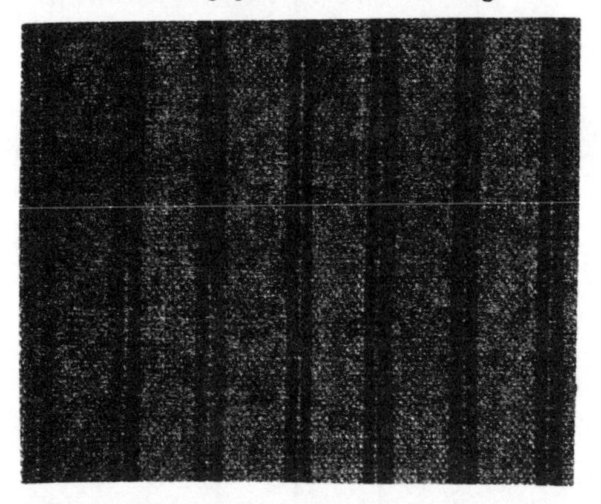

RED AND WHITE TICKING FOR SHIRTING
State Russian Ethnographic Museum, St. Petersburg

RED, WHITE AND BLUE PESTRIADI SHIRT
State Russian Ethnographic Museum, St. Petersburg

RED AND WHITE LINEN PESTRIADI
State Russian Ethnographic Museum, St. Petersburg

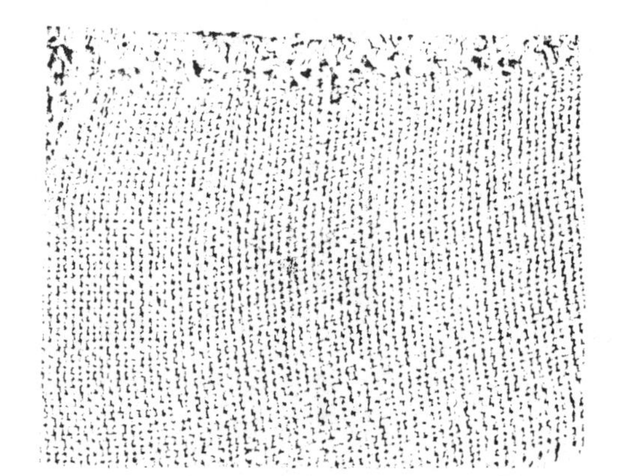

LINEN SHIRTING
State Russian Ethnographic Museum, St. Petersburg

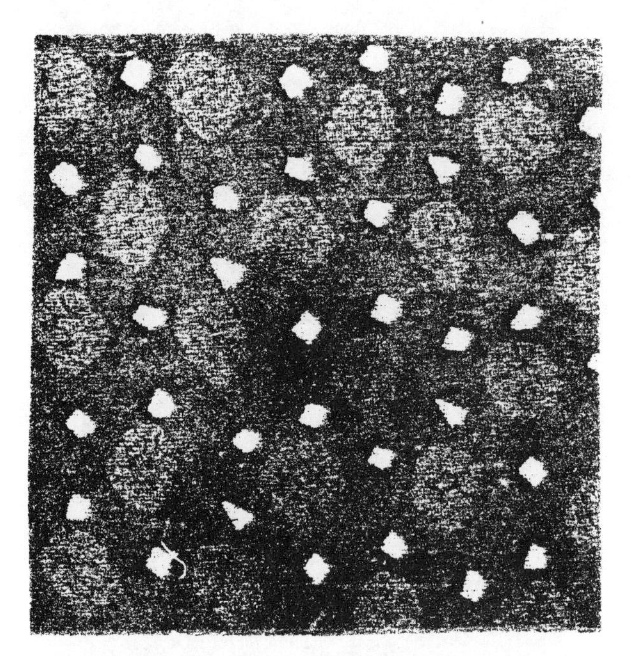

BLUE WITH RED AND WHITE DESIGN COTTON PRINT FOR SKIRTS, 19th Century Russia, Author's Collection

SILK WOVEN MATERIAL FOR DRESSES
19th Century, Russia, FRIA Collection

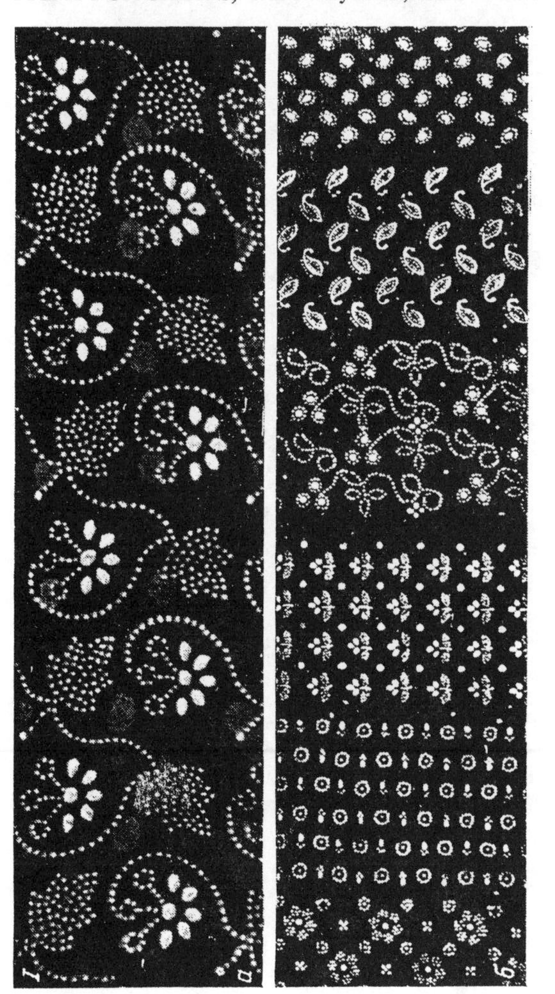

SAMPLES OF CLOTH PRINTED BY BLOCK PRINT METHOD

WOODEN AND METAL BLOCK USED FOR PRINTING

RED, WHITE, DARK AND LIGHT BLUE
PLAID LINEN SKIRT MATERIAL
State Russian Ethnographic Museum, St. Petersburg

RED, WHITE, YELLOW AND BLUE
PLAID LINEN FOR SKIRTS
State Russian Ethnographic Museum, St. Petersburg

RED, WHITE, AND BLACK LINEN TICKING
Novgorod Region, Russia, 19th Century, Author's Collection

LINEN TROUSER BURLAP
State Russian Ethnographic Museum, St. Petersburg

GOLD LACE, 19th Century Russia
State Russian Ethnogaphic Museum , St. Petersburg

REFERENCES

ALEKSANDROV, V. A., et. al.
ETNOGRAFIIA RUSSKOGO KREST'IANSTVA SIBIRI XVII. "Nauka", Moscow, 1981.
NA PUTIAKH IZ ZEMLI PERMSKOI V SIBIR. "Nauka", Moscow, 1989.

ALEKSEEV, A. I.
THE ODYSSEY OF A RUSSIAN SCIENTIST: I. G. VOZNESENSKII IN ALASKA, CALIFORNIA AND SIBERIA, 1839-1849, edited by Richard A. Pierce. The Limestone Press, Kingston, Ontario, 1987.

BASANOFF, V.
ARCHIVES OF THE RUSSIAN CHURCH IN ALASKA, *PACIFIC HISTORICAL REVIEW, VOL. II,* 1933.

BELCHER, EDWARD
H.M.S. SULPHUR ON THE NORTHWEST AND CALIFORNIA COASTS, 1837 AND 1839; ACCOUNTS OF CAPTAIN EDWARD BELCHER AND MIDSHIPMAN FRANCIS GUILLEMARD SIMPKINSON. The Limestone Press, Kingston,Ontario, 1979.

BLACK, LYDIA
ALEUT ART. Aang Angagin: Aleutian/Pribilof Islands Association, Anchorage, Alaska, 1982.

BLASCHKE, EDWARD
MEDICAL TOPOGRAPHY OF THE PORT OF NEW ARCHANGEL, 1842.

BROMLEI, Y. V.
ETHNOGRAPHY OF EASTERN SLAVS. "Nauka", Moscow, *1987.*

DANA, R. H.
TWO YEARS BEFORE THE MAST, A PERSONAL NARRATIVE AT SEA. Two World Publishing Co., Cleveland and New York, 1946.

FEDOROVA, S. G.
THE RUSSIAN POPULATION IN ALASKA AND CALIFORNIA, LATE 18TH CENTURY - 1867 translated and edited by Richard A. Pierce and Alton S. Donnelly. The Limestone Press, Kingston, Ontario, 1973.
PROBLEMII ISTORII I ETNOGRAFII AMERIKI (RUSSKAIA AMERIKA I TOT'MA V SUD'BE IVANA KUSKOVA) translated by Stephen Watrous. "Nauka", Moscow, 1979.

FITZHUGH, WILLIAM W. AND CROWELL, ARON
CROSSROADS OF CONTINENTS. Smithsonian Institution Press, Blue Ridge Summit, Pennsylvania, 1988.

GOLOVNIN, V. M.
AROUND THE WORLD ON THE KAMCHATKA, 1817-1819. The University of Hawaii Press, Honolulu, Hawaii, 1979.

GONCHAROVA, N.N., et al
DLIA PAMIATI POTOMSTVU SVOEMU. Galaktika Art, Moscow, 1993.

HARMUTH, LOUIS
DICTIONARY OF TEXTILES. Fairchild Publishing Company, New York, New York, 1915.

KHLEBNIKOV, K. T.
COLONIAL RUSSIAN AMERICA, KYRILL T. KHLEBNIKOV'S REPORTS, 1817-1832, translated by Basil Dmytryshyn and E. A. P. Crownhart-Vaughan. Oregon Historical Society, Portland, Oregon, 1976.
THE KHLEBNIKOV ARCHIVE, UNPUBLISHED JOURNAL (1800-1837) AND TRAVEL NOTES (1820, 1822, AND 1824), edited by Leonid Shur. University of Alaska Press, Fairbanks, Alaska, 1988.
NOTES ON RUSSIAN AMERICA, PART I: NOVO-ARKHANGEL'SK, compiled by Svetlana G. Fedorova, translated by Serge LeComte and Richard Pierce, edited by Richard Pierce. The Limestone Press, Kingston, Ontario and Fairbanks, Alaska, 1994.

LITKE, F. P.
A VOYAGE AROUND THE WORLD 1826-1829, edited by Richard A. Pierce. The Limestone Press, Kingston, Ontario, 1987.

MALYSHEV, V. N.
UNPUBLISHED TRANSCRIPT OF INTERVIEW ON MERCHANT CLASS STRUCTURE. Fort Ross State Historic Park, California, 1991.
UNPUBLISHED NOTES OF INTERVIEW ON RUSSIAN CLOTHING, 1991. Author's collection.

MONTGOMERY, FLORENCE M.
TEXTILES IN AMERICA 1650-1870. W. W. Norton & Company, New York (A Winterthur/Barra Book), 1984.

OLEKSA, MICHAEL J.
THE CREOLES AND THEIR CONTRIBUTIONS TO THE DEVELOPMENT OF ALASKA in *RUSSIAN AMERICA: THE FORGOTTEN FRONTIER*, edited by Barbara Sweetland Smith and Redmond J. Barnett. Washington State Historical Society, Tacoma, Washington, 1990.

PETROV, V.
RUSSIANS IN AMERICAN HISTORY. Hermitage, New Jersey, 1988.

PIERCE, RICHARD A.
RUSSIAN AMERICA: A BIOGRAPHICAL DICTIONARY. The Limestone Press, Kingston, Ontario, 1990.
THE RUSSIAN-AMERICAN COMPANY, CORRESPONDENCE OF THE GOVERNORS, COMMUNICATIONS SENT: 1818. The Limestone Press, Kingston, Ontario, 1984.
DOCUMENTS ON THE HISTORY OF THE RUSSIAN-AMERICAN COMPANY. Translated by Marina Ramsay. The Limestone Press, Kingston, Ontario, 1976.

PLUMMER, K.
A JAPANESE GLIMPSE AT THE OUTSIDE WORLD 1839-1842 THE TRAVELS OF JIROKICHI IN HAWAII, SIBERIA, AND ALASKA edited by Richard A. Pierce. The Limestone Press, Kingston, Ontario, 1991.

RAY, DOROTHY JEAN
ALEUT AND ESKIMO ART: TRADITION AND INNOVATION IN SOUTH ALASKA. University of Washington Press, Seattle, Washington, 1981.

RUSSIAN EMPIRE
POLNOE SOBRANIE ZAKONOV, 1851. St. Petersburg, Russia.

RYNDINA, V.
RUSSKII KOSTIUM 1830-1850 VYPUSK V'TOROI, translations by Oleg Terichow. Vserossiskoe Teatral'noe Obshchestvo, Moscow, 1961.

SAFARALIEVA, DILIARA
ATTIRES OF THE CALIFORNIA INDIANS IN THE FIRST QUARTER OF THE 19TH CENTURY in *FRIA NEWSLETTER.* Fort Ross, California, 1992.

SERGEEV, M. D., GONCHAROVA, N. N., and SEREBRIAKOV, A. F.
DECEMBRISTS IN SIBERIA. Soviet Russia Publishers, Moscow, 1988.

SHERATON, THOMAS
UPHOLSTERER AND GENERAL ARTIST'S ENCYCLOPEDIA. London, England, 1804-1807.

SMITH, BARBARA SWEETLAND and BARNETT, REDMOND J.
RUSSIAN AMERICA: THE FORGOTTEN FRONTIER. Washington State Historical Society, Tacoma, Washington, 1990.

THOMAS, ROBERT H. G.
THE RUSSIAN ARMY OF THE CRIMEAN WAR 1854-1856, edited by Martin Windrow. Osprey Publishing Ltd., London, 1991.

TORTORA, PHYLLIS and EUBANK, KEITH
A SURVEY OF HISTORIC COSTUME. Fairchild Publications, New York, 1989.

TOZER, JANE and LEVITT, SARAH
FABRIC OF SOCIETY: A CENTURY OF PEOPLE AND THEIR CLOTHES 1770-1870.
Laura Ashley, Ltd., Carno, Powys, Wales, 1983.

TROYAT, H.
DAILY LIFE IN RUSSIA UNDER THE LAST TSAR, translated by Malcolm Barnes. Stanford University Press, California, 1979.

VARJOLA, PIRJO
THE ETHOLEN COLLECTION. National Board of Antiquities, Finland, 1990.

VELTRE, DOUGLAS W.
PERSPECTIVES ON ALEUT CULTURE CHANGE DURING THE RUSSIAN PERIOD in *RUSSIAN AMERICA: FORGOTTEN FRONTIER*, edited by Barbara Sweetland Smith and Redmond J. Barnett. Washington State Historical Society, Tacoma, Washington, 1990.

VON WRANGEL, FERDINAND
RUSSIAN AGENCIES. BARON FERDINAND VON WRANGEL'S REPORT OF APRIL 10, 1834 TO THE MAIN OFFICE, NO. 61 in *RUSSIAN-AMERICAN COMPANY CORRESPONDENCE OF THE GOVERNORS, COMMUNICATIONS SENT: 1834.*
National Archives, (vol. 11, roll no. 36, pp. 59-78).

WERLICH, R.
RUSSIAN ORDERS, DECORATIONS AND MEDALS. Quaker Press, Washington, D.C, 1981.

ZAGOSKIN, L. A.
LIEUTENANT ZAGOSKIN'S TRAVELS IN RUSSIAN AMERICA 1842-1844, edited by Henry N. Michael. The Arctic Institute of North America, University of Toronto Press, 1967.

ZLATICH, MARKO
UNPUBLISHED LETTER TO WAYNE A. COLWELL. Fort Ross State Historic Park, California, 1963.

ILLUSTRATIONS

7 "Settlement Ross", I. G. Voznesenskii, 1841. Original in Peter the Great Museum of Anthropology and Ethnography, Kunstkammer, St. Petersburg, Russia.

10 Decembrists by N. A. Bestuzhev. Original painting in Hermitage Museum, St. Petersburg, Russia.

11 "Portrait of Alexander Baranov", lithograph after an oil by Mikhail T. Tikhanov.*
Civil service uniforms, V. Kozlinskii, inkwash drawing. From Ryndina, V., *Russkii Kostium 1830-1850, vypusk v'toroi*, 1961. Vserossiskoe Teatral'noe Obshchestovo, Moscow.

12 Portraits of Ivan A. Kuskov and Ekaterina P.Kuskova, artist unknown, oil on cardboard. Originals in Tot'ma Regional History Museum, Russia.

13 "Portrait of Merchant with Two Medals on the Neck", V. A. Tropinin, 1838. Original in private collection, Russia.

14 Portraits of Baroness Elizabeth von Wrangell and Governor Ferdinand P. von Wrangell*

15 Portrait of L. A. Hagemeister, artist unknown, oil on canvas.*
Portrait of Margreth Etholen, J. E. Lindh, 1839, oil on canvas.*
Portrait of Governor Arvid A. Etholen, artist unknown, oil on canvas.*

16 "At the Castle", ink on paper, watercolor, Jirokichi, 1842.*

18 "A Creole, California", I. G. Voznesenskii, 1841.* Original drawing in Museum of Anthropology and Ethnography, St. Petersburg, Russia.

19 "Sitka Inhabitant", Jirokichi, 1842.*

20 "Feminine Styles", Jirokichi, 1842.*

21 "Rural Sitka", Friedrich H.von Kittlitz, 1828* Original in *Litke Atlas*.
Illustration of a townswoman, V. Kozlinskii, ink drawing. From Ryndina, V., *Russkii Kostium 1830-1850, vypusk v'toroi,* 1961. Vserossiskoe Teatral'noe Obshchestovo, Moscow.

22 "Sitka, Items of Daily Use (Men's Shirts), Jirokichi, 1842.*
Buttons from cemetery restoration, ink drawing, J. Middleton, 1993.

24 "View of the Russian Capital" (Sitka), F. H. von Kittlitz, 1827* Original in Litke, *Atlas*.

25 "The Forge", L. Plakov, 1845. Original in Russian Museum, St. Petersburg, Russia.

26 "Pacific Islander", Pavel Mikhailov, 1827, pencil.* Original drawing in State Russian Museum, St. Petersburg, Russia.
"Killing a Goat", Jirokichi, 1842.*

27 "Sailor's Outfits, Sitka Drifters", Jirokichi, 1842.*

28 "Drifters in Sailor's Outfits", Jirokichi, 1842.*
"Pacific Islander", Pavel Mikhailov, 1827, pencil* Original drawing in State Russian Museum, St. Petersburg, Russia.

29 Detail of Russian braid, author's collection.
Ceremonial kamleika, Etholen Collection, Helsinki.
Gut cap, Aleut, Pribilof Islands, Etholen collection, Helsinki.
Gut skin cape in Russian style, MAE, St. Petersburg.

30 "Sitka Inhabitants", Jirokichi, 1842.*

31 "Sunday on Unalaska", I. G. Voznesenskii, 1843 and "Cape Espenberg, Kotzebue Sound", I. G. Voznesenskii, 1843* Original drawings in Museum of Anthropology and Ethnography, St. Petersburg, Russia.

32 "Inhabitants of Unalaska", F. H. von Kittlitz, 1828* Original in Litke, *Atlas*.

33 "Young Girls", Pavel Mikhailov, 1827, pencil* Original drawing in State Russian Museum, St. Petersburg, Russia.

34 "California Indians Telling Fortunes", L. Choris. Original in *Voyage pittoresque autour du mond.*

35 "Hunters, Kamchatka", F. H. von Kittlitz, 1827* Original in Litke, *Atlas*.
"Inhabitant of Rumiantsev Bay", Mikhail T. Tikhanov, 1818, watercolor. Original in I. Repin Academy of Fine Arts, St. Petersburg, Russia.

36 "Algarum Vegetatio", A. F. Postels, 1827. Original in *Illustrationes Algarum*, Postels and Ruprecht, in Beinecke Library, Yale University.

37 F. P. von Wrangell*
O. E. Kotzebue*

38 M. P. Lazarev*
"Algarum Vegetatio" (detail), A.F. Postels, 1827.

39 "Sailors at a Bootmakers", A.Denisov, 1832. Original in Russian Museum, St. Petersburg, Russia.

40 "Men of Vostok and Mirnyi in New Zealand", Pavel Mikhailov, 1820 and Untitled, Pavel Mikhailov, 1820* Original drawings in State Russian Museum, St. Petersburg, Russia.

41 Captain-Lieutenant V. A. Kornilov, Karl Briullov, 1836.
M. N. Vasil'ev*

42 V. M. Golovnin*
A. A. Etholen*

45 Decembrists, N. A. Bestuzhev. Original in Hermitage Museum, St. Petersburg, Russia.

46 "Decembrists at the Gate of Fort Chita in Winter," N. P. Repin, 1828-1830. Original in Hermitage Museum, St. Petersburg, Russia.

47 "Portrait of a Merchant in Provincial Merchant Uniform", Kalashnikov, 1840's. *Dlia pamiati potomstvu svoemu,* 1993. Galaktika Art, Moscow.

48 Reconstruction of Russian civil service uniform, townsman and worker, Viktor N. Malyshev, 1991.

49 Order of St. Anna, court sword and Medal for Zealous Service, all from State History Museum, Moscow.

50 Civil ministries uniform, 1830's, V. Kozlinskii. Ryndina, V., *Russkii Kostium 1830-1850, vypusk vtoroi.* 1961. Vserossiskoe Teatral'noe Obshchestvo, Moscow.

51 Views of Decembrists, N. P. Repin, 1828-1830. Originals in the Hermitage Museum, St. Petersburg, Russia.

52-57 Views of Decembrists, N. A. Bestuzhev, 1830's. Originals in the Hermitage Museum, St. Petersburg, Russia.

58-59 Views of Decembrist ladies, various artists, 1820's to1840's. Originals in the Hermitage Museum.

60 "Portrait of P. A. Spasskii", 1829, N. D. Myl'nikov. Goncharova, N.N., et al. *Dlia pamiati potomstvu svoemu,* 1993. Galaktika Art, Moscow.

61 "Portrait of a Merchant's Wife", artist unknown, 1830's. Goncharova, N.N., et al. *Dlia pamiati potomstvu svoemu,* 1993. Galaktika Art, Moscow.

62 “Portrait of a Merchant’s Wife A. B. Dvornikov”, N. T. Durnov, 1829. Goncharova, N.N., et al. *Dlia pamiati potomstvu svoemu,* 1993. Galaktika Art, Moscow.

63 “Portrait of the Artist’s Daughters”, Evgraf Krendovskii, 1845. Original in Taganrog Art Gallery, Russia.
“Portrait Nasten’ka Khavshaia”, A. Venetsianov, 1826. Original in Venetsianov Art Museum, Archangelsk, Russia.

64 “Portrait of Panaev Children”, A. Venetsianov, 1841. Original in Tretyakov Gallery, Moscow.
“Study in the House at Ostrovki” (detail), Grigory Soroka, 1844. Original in Russian Museum, St. Petersburg, Russia.
“Portrait of Senator A. Bashilov and the Children of Court De Balmaine”, Evgraf Krendovskii. Original in Tretyakov Gallery, Moscow.

65 Decembrist children, A. Manyani. Originals in the Hermitage Museum, St. Petersburg, Russia.

66 “Portrait of the Merchant Family Kosinikh at Tea”, Kuchikov, 1840’s. Goncharova, N.N., et al. *Dlia pamiati potomstvu svoemu,* 1993. Galaktika Art, Moscow.

67 Townsman and woman, V. Kozlinskii, ink drawing. Ryndina, V., *Russkii Kostium 1830-1850, vypusk v'toroi.* 1961. Vserossiskoe Teatral’noe Obshchestovo, Moscow.

68 “Townspeople in the Forest”, A. Shchokhin, 1840. Goncharova, N.N., et al. *Dlia pamiati potomstvu svoemu,* 1993. Galaktika Art, Moscow.

69 Painted spruce root hat, Tlingit, Etholen Collection Helsinki.
19th century spruce root hats collected by Russians. Originals in Peter the Great Museum of Anthropology and Ethnography, St. Petersburg, Russia

70 A townsman in work clothing, J. Middleton, 1993.

71 Man’s woolen vest, 1840’s, illustrated in Goncharova, N.N., et al. *Dlia pamiati potomstvu svoemu,* 1993. Galaktika Art, Moscow.

72 A creole in office clothing, J. Middleton, 1993.

73 Kerchiefs, Moscow Province, late 18th - early 19th centuries. State History Museum, Moscow, Russia.

74 A woman of the townsman class, J. Middleton, 1993.

75 Shawl (detail), 1840's, Guchkov Factory, Moscow. State History Museum, Moscow, Russia.

76 Everyday dress of townswoman, J. Middleton, 1993.

77 Townsman's coat, ink drawing, V. Kozlinskii. Ryndina, V., *Russkii kostium 1830-1850, vypusk v'toroi.* 1961. Vserossiskoe Teatral'noe Obshchestovo, Moscow.

78 "Dunya, the Stationmaster's Daughter", M. V. Dobuzhinsky, first half 19th century. Original in Stationmaster's Watchhouse Museum, Vyra, St. Petersburg Province, Russia.

79 "Kitchen", Gury Krylov, 1826-27. Original in Russian Museum, St. Petersburg, Russia.

80 "The Lacemaker", V. A. Tropinin, 1823. Original in Tretyakov Gallery, Moscow, Russia.
"Lacemaking", V. A. Tropinin, 1830. Original in private collection, Moscow, Russia.

81 "Girl With a Pot of Roses", V. A. Tropinin, 1850. Original in Tropinin Museum, Moscow, Russia.

82 "Girl With a Dog", V. A. Tropinin, 1820's -1830's. Original in Tropinin Museum, Moscow, Russia.
"Girl Wearing a Shawl", A. Venetsianov, 1830. Original in Venetsianov Museum, St. Petersburg, Russia.

83 "Boy Releasing a Goldfinch", V. A. Tropinin, 1825. Original in Regional Art Museum, Ivanova, Russia.
"Girl with a Doll", V. A. Tropinin, 1841. Russian Museum, St. Petersburg, Russia.

84 "View of Rural Sitka", F. H. von Kittlitz, 1828* Original in *Litke Atlas.*

85 "Portrait of Merchant", V. D'iakonov, 1836. Goncharova, N.N., et al. *Dlia pamiati potomstvu svoemu,* 1993. Galaktika Art, Moscow.

86 Merchant and company employee, Viktor N. Malyshev, 1991.

87 Hunting kamleika, Etholen Collection, Helsinki.

88 Aleut employee in the working clothes of the 1830's, J. Middleton, 1993.

89 Resist print fabric, author's collection.

90 An employee's wife, J. Middleton, 1993.

91 Company sailor, 1851. Russian Empire, *Polnoe sobranie zakonov*. 1851. St. Petersburg, Russia.

92 Company employee in "festive dress", J. Middleton, 1993.

93-96 *Na putiakh iz zemli Permskoi v Sibir.*
Ethnography of Eastern Slavs
Etnografiia russkogo krest'ianstva Sibiri XVII.
Victor Malyshev, State Artillery History Museum.
Olga Zaitseva from Kizhi Museum Collection.
John Middleton after Victor Malyshev, State Artillery History Museum.

97 "Sitka Harbor (detail), artist unknown.*

98 "Kronshtadt Road", I. K. Aivazovsky, 1840. Original in Central Naval Museum, St. Petersburg, Russia.

99 Naval buttons, first half 19th century, author's collection.
Boatswain's whistle, first half 19th century, reproduced from undated 19th century naval uniform manual, courtesy of Victor Malyshev.

100 Sailors, Viktor N. Malyshev, 1991.

101 - 102 1851 published regulations for ship's uniforms of the Russian-American Company. Russian Empire, *Polnoe sobranie zakonov*. 1851. St. Petersburg, Russia.

103 "Oarsmen from the Cutter of the 3rd Naval Division, 1843". Original in the Central Naval Museum, St. Petersburg, Russia.

104 Sailor, reconstruction from a Pavel Mikhailov drawing, Viktor N. Malyshev, 1991.

105 Naval clothing reproduced from undated 19th century naval uniform manual, courtesey of Victor N. Malyshev.

106 - 110 Naval clothing, reconstructions from collections in the State Artillery History Museum, St. Petersburg, Viktor N. Malyshev, 1991.

113 - 116 Photographs from Fort Ross Cemetery Restoration Project, 1991, Alan Magayne-Roshak.

*Reprints courtesy Limestone Press

THE LIMESTONE PRESS
ALASKA HISTORY SERIES

1. R.A. Pierce, **ALASKA SHIPPING, 1867-1878. ARRIVALS AND DEPARTURES AT THE PORT OF SITKA**, 1972. 72 pp., illus. Shipping at the end of the Russian regime and during the first decade of American rule.
2. F.W. Howay. **A LIST OF TRADING VESSELS IN THE MARITIME FUR TRADE, 1785-1825.** 1973. 209 pp., bibliog., index. Fundamental work on early Northwest Coast.
3. K.T. Khlebnikov, **LIFE OF BARANOV**. 1973. 140 pp., illus., index. Biog. of the first governor of the Russian colonies in America. Tr. of Russ. ed. of 1835. OUT OF PRINT
4. S.G. Fedorova. **THE RUSSIAN POPULATION IN ALASKA AND CALIFORNIA, LATE 18th CENTURY TO 1867.** 1973. 367 pp., illus., maps, index. Tr. of Russ. ed. of 1971. OUT OF PRINT.
5. V.N. Berkh. **A CHRONOLOGICAL HISTORY OF THE DISCOVERY OF THE ALEUTIAN ISLANDS**. 1974. 121 pp., illus., maps, index. Tr. of Russ. ed. of 1823. OUT OF PRINT
6. R.V. Makarova. **RUSSIANS ON THE PACIFIC,** 1743-1799. 1975 301 pp., illus., maps, index. Tr. of Russ. ed. of 1968. OUT OF PRINT
7. **DOCUMENTS ON THE HISTORY OF THE RUSSIAN-AMERICAN COMPANY.** 1976. 220 pp., illus., maps, index. Tr. of Russ. ed. of 1957
8. R.A. Pierce, **RUSSIA'S HAWAIIAN ADVENTURE**, 1815-1817. 245 pp., illus., maps, index. Reprint of 1965 ed.
9. H.W. Elliott. **THE SEAL ISLANDS OF ALASKA.** Reprint of the 1881 edition, prepared for the Tenth Census of the United States. 176 pp., large format, many illustrations.
10. G.I. Davydov. **TWO VOYAGES TO RUSSIAN AMERICA, 1802-1807.** 1977. 257 pp., illus., maps, index. Transl. of the Russ. ed. of 1810-1812. Travel, history and ethnography in Siberia and Alaska.
11. **THE RUSSIAN ORTHODOX RELIGIOUS MISSION IN AMERICA, 1794-1807.** 1977. 257 pp., illus., index. 186 pp. Tr. of the Russ. ed. of 1894. Documents on the mission and life of its most famous member, the monk German (St. Herman), with ethnographic notes on the Kodiak islanders and Aleuts by the hiermonk Gedeon. OUT OF PRINT.
12. **H.M.S. SULPHUR ON THE NORTHWEST AND CALIFORNIA COASTS, 1837 AND 1839.** Accounts by Capt. Edward Belcher and Midshipman G. Simpkinson, concerning native peoples of Russian America and California. 1979. 144 pp., illus., maps.
13. P.A. Tikhmenev. **A HISTORY OF THE RUSSIAN-AMERICAN COMPANY**. Vol. 2: **DOCUMENTS**. Appendices to a classic account. (V. 1 publ. by U. of Washington Press, 1978). Tr. of the Russ. edition of 1861-1863. OUT OF PRINT
14. N.A. Ivashintsov. **RUSSIAN ROUND-THE-WORLD VOYAGES, 1803-1849**. 156 pp., illus., maps. Tr. by Glynn Barratt from Russ. ed. of 1849, with additional list of voyages to 1867. Summaries, based on logs, indicating ports of call, activities and personnel. Essential for several fields of research. Illus.
15. Wrangell, Baron Ferdinand von. **RUSSIAN AMERICA, STATISTICAL AND ETHNOGRAPHIC INFORMATION ON THE RUSSIAN POSSESSIONS ON THE NORTHWEST COAST OF AMERICA**. Tr. of the German ed., publ. in St. P., 1839. 1980. 204 pp. OUT OF PRINT
16. **THE JOURNAL OF IAKOV NETSVETOV: THE ATKA YEARS, 1828-1844.** Transl. by Lydia Black of the unpubl. manuscript, with notes and supplements on the history and ethnography of the Aleutian Islands. 1980. 340 pp. OUT OF PRINT
17. **SIBERIA AND NORTHWESTERN AMERICA, 1788-1792. THE JOURNAL OF CARL HEINRICH MERCK, NATURALIST WITH THE RUSSIAN SCIENTIFIC EXPEDITION LED BY CAPTAIN JOSEPH BILLINGS AND GAVRILL SARYCHEV.** Tr. by Fritz Jaensch from the unpub. Ger. manuscript. Includes ethnographic, biological and geological observations. Illus., maps, index, 1980. OUT OF PRINT
18. David Hunter Miller. **THE ALASKA TREATY**. 1981. 221 pp., detailed study of the Alaska purchase, prepared in 1944 for the U.S. Dept. of State's Treaty Series, but not published.
19. G.I. Shelikhov. **VOYAGE TO AMERICA, 1783-1785**. 1981. 162 pp., illus., maps, index, supplementary materials. Tr. of Russ. ed. of 1812. Includes Shelikhov's book, publ in 1791, with materials erroneously attributed to him since early 19th century. OUT OF PRINT
20. **KODIAK AND AFOGNAK LIFE**, 1868-1870. The journals of Lts. E.L. Huggins and John Campbell, and merchant Frederick Sargent, with other materials relating to the first years of the American regime in Alaska, including portraits, and early map of Kodiak. Details on ship movements, personnel, trade and life style. 1981. 163 pp. OUT OF PRINT
21. M.D. Teben'kov. **ATLAS OF THE NORTHWEST COASTS OF AMERICA FROM BERING STRAIT TO CAPE CORRIENTES AND THE ALEUTIAN ISLANDS WITH SEVERAL SHEETS ON THE NORTHEAST COAST OF ASIA**. Compiled by Teben'kov while governor of Russian America, and publ. in

1852. 39 sheets, boxed with softbound vol. With rare **HYDROGRAPHIC NOTES** (109 pp.) and supplementary information. 1981.

22. G.R. Adams. **LIFE ON THE YUKON, 1865-1867.** 1982. 219 pp., illus. From ms. diary of a participant in the Western Union Telegraph Expedition, and later autobiographical account.
23. Dorothy Jean Ray. **ETHNOHISTORY IN THE ARCTIC: THE BERING STRAIT ESKIMO.** Articles, assembled in one volume for the first time, on early trade, the legendary 17th century Russian settlement, the history of St. Michael, Eskimo picture writing, land tenure and polity, settlement and subsistence patterns, and place names. Tr. of Russ. accounts of the Vasil'ev-Shishmarev expedition (1819-1822). 280 pp., illus., maps. OUT OF PRINT
24. Lydia Black. **ATKA. AN ETHNOHISTORY OF THE WESTERN ALEUTIANS. 1984.** 219 pp., illus. Problems of prehistory, ethnography, and 18th century foreign contacts, with a list of Russian voyages, the account of navigator Vasil'ev (1811-1812), Fr. Ioann Veniaminov, and biographical materials.
25. **THE RUSSIAN-AMERICAN COMPANY. THE CORRESPONDENCE OF THE GOVERNORS. COMMUNICATIONS SENT: 1818.** 1984. xiv. 194 pp., index, notes. Tr. of ms. material in U.S. National Archives.
26. **THE JOURNALS OF IAKOV NETSVETOV: THE YUKON YEARS, 1845-1863**. 1984. 505 pp., illus., maps. Tr. by Lydia Black from unpub. ms. in Library of Congress, with notes and appendices on history and ethnography of the Yukon and Kuskokwim regions of Alaska.
27. Ioann Veniaminov. (St. Innokentii). **NOTES ON THE ISLANDS OF THE UNALASHKA DISTRICT**. 1985. 511 pp., illus. Tr. of Russ. ed., St.P., 1840.
28. R.A. Pierce. **BUILDERS OF ALASKA: THE RUSSIAN GOVERNORS**, 1818-1867. Biographies of Alaska's 13 forgotten governors, from Hagemeister to Maksutov. 1986. 53 pp., illus.
29. Frederic Litke: **A VOYAGE AROUND THE WORLD, 1826-1829. Vol 1: TO RUSSIAN AMERICA AND SIBERIA, 1839-1849.** Tr. of French ed. (Paris, 1835) by R. Marshall; with a parallel account by F.H. Baron von Kittlitz, tr. by V.J. Moessner from the German ed. of 1854. 1987. 232 pp., maps, illus.
30. A.I. Alekseev. **THE ODYSSEY OF A RUSSIAN SCIENTIST: I.G. VOZNESENSKII IN ALASKA CALIFORNIA AND SIBERIA, 1839-1849**,. Tr. of the Russ. ed. (M., 1977), by Wilma C. Follette. Edited by R.A. Pierce. 1988. 130 pp., illus., maps.
31. Ann Fienup-Riordan, ed. **THE YUP'IK ESKIMO AS DESCRIBED IN THE TRAVEL JOURNALS AND ETHNOGRAPHIC ACCOUNTS OF JOHN AND EDITH KILBUCK, 1885-1900.** 1988. vii + 528 pp., illus., maps. OUT OF PRINT
32. **THE ROUND THE WORLD VOYAGE OF HIEROMONK GIDEON, 1803-1809.** Tr., with intro. and notes, by Lydia T. Black. 1989. xiii+ 184 pp., illus., maps.
33. R.A. Pierce. **RUSSIAN AMERICA: A BIOGRAPHICAL DICTIONARY**. 1990. xxii.+ 570pp.
34. A.I. Alekseev. **THE DESTINY OF RUSSIAN AMERICA**. Tr. by Marina Ramsay of the Russ. ed. of 1975. 1990. x + 341 pp., illus.
35. **RUSSIA IN NORTH AMERICA. PROCEEDINGS OF THE 2D INTERNATIONAL CONFERENCE ON RUSSIAN AMERICA**, Sitka, Alaska, August 19-22, 1987. 1990. x + 527 pp., illus.
36. Katherine Plummer, ed. **A JAPANESE GLIMPSE AT THE OUTSIDE WORLD, 1839-1843. THE TRAVELS OF JIROKICHI IN HAWAII, SIBERIA AND ALASKA**. Adapted from the Japanese. 1991. 182 + 94 pp. of illus.
37. Rhys Richards. **CAPTAIN SIMON METCALFE; PIONEER FUR TRADER IN THE PACIFIC NORTHWEST, HAWAII AND CHINA**, 1787-1794, 234 pp., illus.
38. **THE LOVTSOV ATLAS OF THE NORTH PACIFIC OCEAN, COMPILED AT BOL'SHERETSK, KAMCHATKA, in 1782.** Tr., with introd. and notes, by Lydia Black, from original ms.
39. E.O. Essig, et. al. **FORT ROSS, CALIFORNIA OUTPOST OF RUSSIAN ALASKA, 1812-1841.** Reprint, Quarterly of California Historical Society, Vol. 12:3, San Francisco, September 1933. 106 pp., illus.
40. Roscoe, Fred. **FROM HUMBOLDT TO KODIAK 1886-1895. RECOLLECTIONS OF A FRONTIER CHILDHOOD**. Ed. by Stanley N. Roscoe. Softbound.
41. von Langsdorff, G.H. **REMARKS AND OBSERVATIONS ON A VOYAGE AROUND THE WORLD FROM 1803 TO 1807**. 1993, 2 vols. in 1, illus. Tr. by Joan Moessner from the German ed. of 1812.
42. Khlebnikov, K.T. **NOTES ON RUSSIAN AMERICA. PART 2 (NOVO-ARKHANGEL'SK.).** Transcribed by Roza G. Liapunova and Svetlana Fedorova. Tr. from the Russ. ed. of 1979 by M. Ramsay.
43. Khlebnikov, K.T. **NOTES ON RUSSIAN AMERICA, PART 1: NOVO-ARKHANGEL'SK**. Transcribed by Svetlana Fedorova from the original ms., with extensive notes. Tr. from the Russ. ed. of 1955 by Serge LeComte and R.A. Pierce.
44. Middleton, John **CLOTHING IN COLONIAL RUSSIAN AMERICA: A NEW LOOK**. 1996. 138 p., illus.

45. Bolkhovitinov, N.N. **RUSSIAN-AMERICAN RELATIONS AND THE SALE OF ALASKA, 1834-1867**. 1996. 390 p., illus. Tr. by R.A. Pierce from the Russ. ed., of 1990.

The Rasmuson Library
Historical Translation Series
Marvin W. Falk, Editor

HOLMBERG'S ETHNOGRAPHIC SKETCHES. By Heinrich Johan Holmberg. Edited by Marvin W. Falk. Translated from the original German of 1855-1863 by Fritz Jaensch. RLHTS Volume I, 1985.
TLINGIT INDIANS OF ALASKA. By Archimandrite Anatolii Kamenskii. Translated, with an Introduction and Supplementary Material by Sergei Kan. RLHTS Volume II, 1985.
BERING'S VOYAGES: THE REPORTS FROM RUSSIA. By Gerhard Friedrich Muller. Translated, with commentary by Carol Urness. RLHTS Volume III, 1986.
RUSSIAN EXPLORATION IN SOUTHWEST ALASKA: THE TRAVEL JOURNALS OF PETR KORSAKOVSKIY (1818) AND IVAN YA. VASILEV (1829). Edited with introduction by James W. VanStone. Translated by David H. Kraus. RLHTS Volume IV, 1988.
THE KHLEBNIKOV ARCHIVE. UNPUBLISHED JOURNAL (1800-1837) AND TRAVEL NOTES (1820, 1822, and 1824). Edited, with introduction and notes, by Leonid Shur. Translated by John Bisk. RLHTS Volume V, 1990.
THE GREAT RUSSIAN NAVIGATOR, A.I. CHIRIKOV. By Vasilii A. Divin. Translated and annotated by Raymond H. Fisher. RLHTS Volume VI, 1993.
JOURNALS OF THE PRIEST IOANN VENIAMINOV IN ALASKA, 1823 TO 1836. Introduction and commentary by S.A. Mousalimas. Translated by Jerome Kisslinger. RLHTS Volume VII, 1993.
TO THE CHUKCHI PENINSULA AND TO THE TLINGIT INDIANS 1881/1882. JOURNALS AND LETTERS BY AUREL AND ARTHUR KRAUSE. Translated by Margot Krause McCaffrey. RLHTS Volume VIII, 1993.
ESSAYS ON THE ETHNOGRAPHY OF THE ALEUTS (AT THE END OF THE EIGHTEENTH AND THE FIRST HALF OF THE NINETEENTH CENTURY). By R.G. Liapunova. Translated by Jerry Shelest with the editoral assistance of William B. Workman and Lydia T. Black. RLHTS Volume IX, 1996.
FEDOR PETROVICH LITKE. By A.I. Alekseev. Edited by Katherine L. Arndt. Translated by Sergei Lecomte. RLHTS Volume X, 1996.
NOTES ON THE ISLANDS OF THE UNALASHKA DISTRICT. By Ivan Veniaminov. Translated by Lydia T. Black and R.H. Geoghegan. Edited with an Introduction by Richard A. Pierce. Published jointly by the Elmer E. Rasmuson Library Translation Program and the Limestone Press, 1984.

All titles listed are available from the University of Alaska Press.

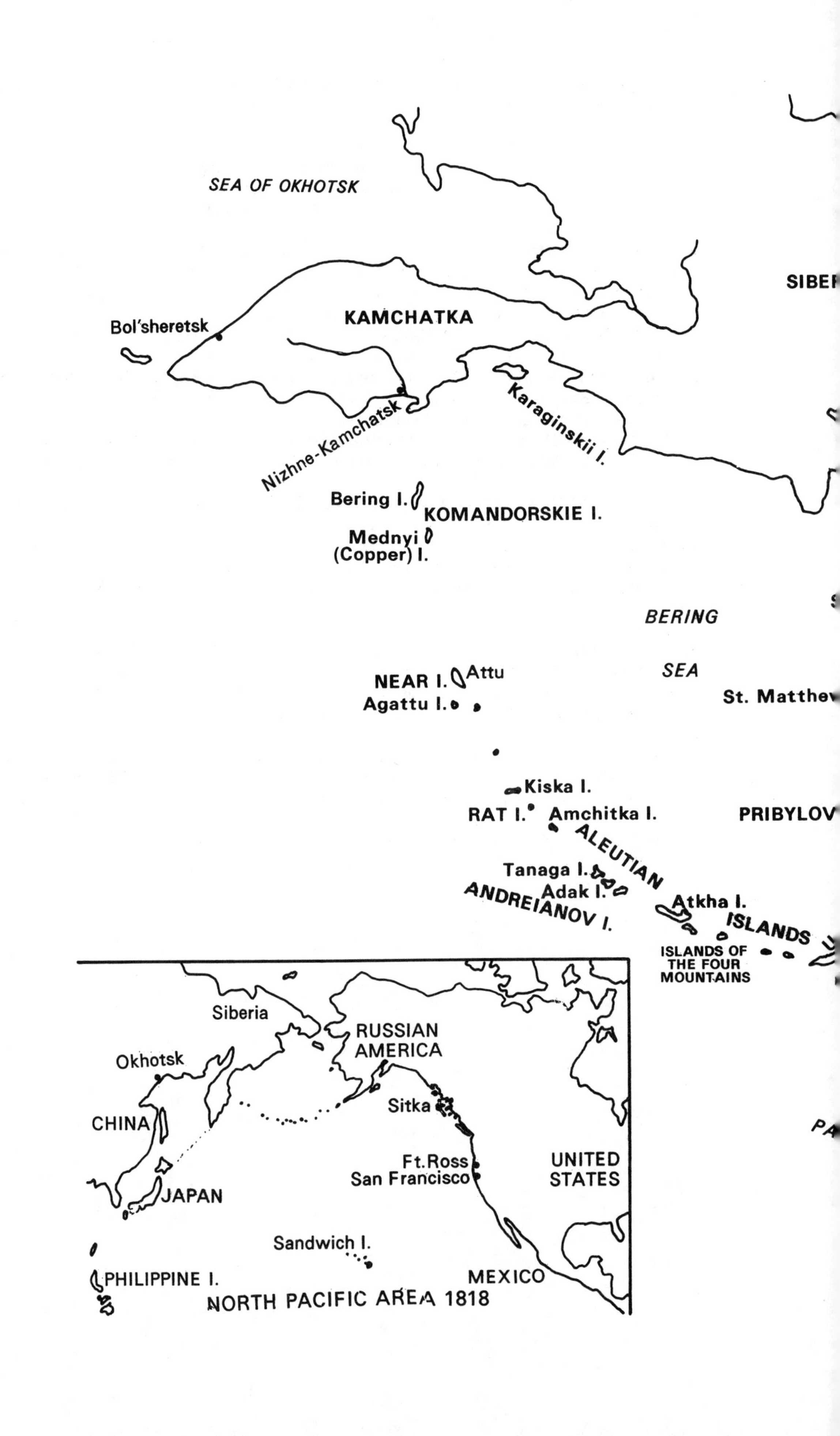
SEA OF OKHOTSK
KAMCHATKA
Bol'sheretsk
Nizhne-Kamchatsk
Karaginskii I.
Bering I.
KOMANDORSKIE I.
Mednyi
(Copper) I.
BERING
SEA
NEAR I.
Attu
Agattu I.
Kiska I.
RAT I.
Amchitka I.
ALEUTIAN
ISLANDS
Tanaga I.
Adak I.
ANDREIANOV I.
Atkha I.
ISLANDS OF
THE FOUR
MOUNTAINS
Siberia
Okhotsk
CHINA
JAPAN
RUSSIAN
AMERICA
Sitka
Ft.Ross
San Francisco
UNITED
STATES
Sandwich I.
MEXICO
PHILIPPINE I.
NORTH PACIFIC AREA 1818

YR
rence I.
nivak I.
Paul I.
George I.
Unimak I.
a I.
SHUMAGIN I.
ALASKA PEN.
L. Iliamna
Kenai Bay
KENAI PEN.
Kodiak I.
Pavlovsk Harbor
(Kodiak)
Yukon R.
Kuskokwim R.
RUSSIAN
AMERICA
Yukon R.
Chugach Bay
Mt.
St. Elias
Nuchek I.
Montague I.
Resurrection Bay
Yakutat Bay
Yakutat
Sitka
(Novo-Arkhangel'sk)
OCEAN